YAMASAKI IN DETROIT

Wayne State University Press gratefully acknowledges the organizations
that generously supported the publication of this book.

Friends of Modern and Contemporary Art, Detroit Institute of Arts

and

Yamasaki, Inc.

The Office of the Vice President of Research (OVPR) of Wayne State University

YAMASAKI IN DETROIT
A Search for Serenity

John Gallagher

A PAINTED TURTLE BOOK
Detroit, Michigan

© 2015 by Wayne State University Press, Detroit, Michigan 48201.
All rights reserved. No part of this book may be reproduced without formal permission.
Manufactured in the United States of America.

19 18 17 16 15   5 4 3 2 1

Library of Congress Control Number: 2015935288

ISBN 978–0-8143-4119-3 (cloth)
ISBN 978–0-8143-4120-9 (ebook)

Published with support from the Regional Book Fund.

Designed and typeset by Bryce Schimanski
Composed in Adobe Caslon Pro and Trade Gothic

To Sheu-Jane, my own source of serenity and delight

CONTENTS

Preface ix

Acknowledgments xi

Life and Work 1

Selected Projects 61

Notes 109

Index 115

PREFACE

This exploration of the life and architecture of Minoru Yamasaki (1912–1986) grew out of a series of events that culminated in 2013. Best known for designing the World Trade Center towers in New York, Yamasaki lived in Detroit most of his career. During the 1950s and '60s, Wayne State University in Detroit commissioned him again and again to do campus design work. Yamasaki produced not only an overall campus plan but also designed four of Wayne State's most iconic buildings—the schools of Business and Education, the delightful DeRoy Auditorium, and the jewel-like McGregor Memorial Conference Center. The latter two projects included outdoor pools, a signature element that Yamasaki used in some of his best work. Over time, drainage problems prompted the university to empty the pools at both DeRoy and McGregor, and the pools remained empty and unsightly for many years. Then, in 2013, Wayne State completed its nearly two million dollar restoration of the pools at McGregor, returning what many observers believe to be Yamasaki's best building to his original vision. It was a triumph of thoughtful preservation.

As the longtime architecture and development writer for the *Detroit Free Press*, I covered the McGregor restoration project for the newspaper. But I found there was appetite for more writing about Minoru Yamasaki. Both the members of an advisory committee on the McGregor restoration and my editors at Wayne State University Press, the publisher of my previous books on architecture and urban planning, were eager for something on Yamasaki. Not that I needed much urging; I had long been a fan of Yamasaki's work. I had arrived in Detroit too late to know him personally; Yama, as he was known by friends and colleagues, died in 1986, a year before I got to town. But I did meet many of his partners and associates and had long enjoyed his elegant modernist works of architecture. I quickly signed on to do a book on Yama and his work.

This book is meant to introduce both knowledgeable fans of architecture and the general reader to a remarkable artist. It is not intended to be an exhaustive study of all his work but rather a survey of his life and work and how they intersected. Yamasaki was one of those rare architects who had developed a unique design philosophy (as distinct from simply following the latest style) and who managed to enact it fairly often during his working life. His design philosophy was not something he learned in school but something that grew out of his life experiences. These included his poverty-ridden childhood in Seattle; the discrimination he faced as a Japanese American during and after World War II; and the burden he placed on himself, as the eldest son of immigrant parents, to succeed in America. All these factors drove Yamasaki to emphasize the serene, the life-enhancing, and the delightful in his architecture. His palette may have been steel and glass, but his values were humanistic to the core.

That Yamasaki's reputation needed some burnishing was another motivation for this book. Because his World Trade Center twin towers proved so unpopular—viewed by many as out of proportion to the rest of Manhattan's skyline—critics over the years have tended to relegate Yamasaki to the second tier in architecture's pantheon. I believed better of Yamasaki and his work; privileged to live near his many projects in his adopted home of Detroit, I understood, perhaps better than some distant critics could, how Yama's architecture worked in person. Only by standing amid one of his projects can one feel the surprise and delight that Yama strove so hard to create.

This book, then, is both a biography of Yamasaki and an examination of his working practices and his search for a style that would express his artistic goals. Yamasaki titled his own autobiographical work *A Life in Architecture*, and my book will demonstrate that Yamasaki lived the life of an architect to the fullest. That life was not always easy. Yamasaki faced many serious health problems, his marital life was troubled, and critics often slammed his work. But the overall judgment on Minoru Yamasaki must be positive, even joyous. As Gunnar Birkerts, who worked for Yama before starting his own independent career, says later in this book, Yamasaki was an architect like we always imagine our architects to be.

ACKNOWLEDGMENTS

The main sources for this study of Minoru Yamasaki's life and career include Yama's own autobiographical book, *A Life in Architecture*, as well as interviews with five architects who worked with Yamasaki in his firm: Henry Guthard, Kip Serota, Gunnar Birkerts, John Suhr, and Keith Brown. The author also wishes to thank the staff of the Reuther Library at Wayne State University, where Yamasaki's correspondence and personal papers are stored; the staff of the Michigan Historic Preservation Office, who made photographs available from their excellent Michigan Modern collection; Christian Korab, son of the renowned architectural photographer Balthazar Korab, for making other images available for this book; and Eric Hill, who with this author co-wrote the *AIA Detroit* guidebook and who shared his perspective on Yamasaki's work in an insightful interview. Other thanks go to the staffs at the State Archives of Michigan, the Birmingham Historical Museum and Park, and the Bancroft Library at the University of California, Berkeley, for making material available; and to SmithGroupJJR, the successor firm to Smith, Hinchman & Grylls, Yama's employer in the late 1940s. As secondary sources, the author found the books *City in the Sky: The Rise and Fall of the World Trade Center*, by James Glanz and Eric Lipton, and *Smith, Hinchman & Grylls: 125 Years of Architecture and Engineering, 1853–1978*, by Thomas J. Holleman and James P. Gallagher, both helpful resources.

LIFE AND WORK

EARLY LIFE

The Yesler Hill district of Seattle, where Minoru Yamasaki was born in 1912, helped give the world the term *skid row*. Not, it seems, for the tenements where the boy's immigrant Japanese parents rented lodgings soon after marrying but for the loggers who used to slide their toppled trees down the slopes in chutes to the waterway below. But the other more common meaning of the word applied, too. The child's parents—who met for the first time in Seattle and married there—at first couldn't afford much better than a tenement apartment perched precariously on a hillside with an outhouse at the rear of the building. But the boy's father, coming from a well-to-do rice-producing family in Japan, burned with initiative. He always had two or three jobs. As his income grew, the father moved his family to better quarters (with hot water and indoor plumbing). Eventually, young Minoru was helping his father clean the floors of a chocolate factory on Sunday mornings—the boy regretting only that he couldn't eat any of the tempting chocolate all around him.

As a boy, Yama liked to slip away from his parents' cold-water flat to bicycle to the countryside. He would linger atop one of the city's hills to take in vistas of the Cascades and the Olympic Mountains, with Mount Rainier to the south and the foam-flecked waters of Puget Sound to the west. He gloried in these Saturday excursions, finding a tranquility and spiritual lift that he would continue to seek throughout his often-troubled life. Even many years later, when his name was celebrated around the globe, he never wavered from his life's mission: to give people what nature had given him.

Standards were high in the Yamasaki household. Minoru skipped a grade in grammar school. His mother kept him practicing the piano for hours against his will. He excelled in his favorite subjects, math and science, and in his senior year of high school, when every high school senior city wide took a mathematics exam,

Yamasaki as a toddler with his parents. (Photo courtesy of Walter P. Reuther Library, Wayne State University)

Minoru was the only one to earn a perfect grade. Nothing less than the many As that he got was expected from the oldest son of an immigrant family on whom so many hopes rested.

Henry Guthard—a young engineering intern when he first met Yama in Detroit and who, over some forty years, rose to be his top aide—saw Yama's drive as stemming from being the oldest son and first child of his immigrant Japanese parents: "Yama was the hope of his family. It was a responsibility that he had and that bore heavily on the shoulders of a little guy growing up. He knew and believed and wanted to satisfy the requirements of helping the family. He felt enormous guilt. He also had enormous insecurity. So everything gained a dimension of need, of need to be as perfect as possible, and he carried that into his architecture. . . . This attention to detail became so important to him that it almost overwhelmed him."

It was in his teen years that the lad, brilliant but unfocused and interested in girls and baseball, found his calling. His uncle, Koken Ito, his mother's brother, visited the family in Seattle after graduating in architecture from the University of California. Ito unrolled some drawings he had made at the university, and Minoru discovered his own future. "I almost exploded with excitement when I saw them," he would write decades later. "Right then and there I decided to become an architect, and I have been steadfast in that resolution ever since."

Despite that goal, Yama, as friends and coworkers would know him, considered skipping college in favor of working for a local branch of a large Japanese firm. He was dating the daughter of a Japanese family, who was, like himself, a Nisei, as first-generation Japanese immigrant children were known. He wanted to earn the money to buy his own car. Independence beckoned. But his father browbeat his son into dropping the idea and even breaking up with his girlfriend, in order to concentrate on his studies. Decades later, Yama recalled how disconsolate he had felt, but he agreed that his father had been right. Breaking up with his girlfriend was an early price he would pay for success, but it wouldn't be the last.

Yama entered the University of Washington to study architecture and soon learned that he had had little preparation. Abashed by his lack of drawing skills, he worked hard at improving and soon received an A for his watercolors. But he struggled between his love of the arts and the necessity for engineering skills. Finally, he consulted a professor named Lionel Pries, who talked the uncertain student out of quitting, telling Yama that he would be among the best architects to ever graduate from the school. Buoyed by this show of confidence, Yama drove ahead with renewed energy.

Those were the Depression years. During summers at college, Yama had to work at any job he could find. That turned out to be laboring in salmon canneries along the Alaskan coast. His coworkers were other Nisei and a few Filipinos, evidently the only ones willing to accept the low pay and terrible conditions. The first month was spent readying the cannery, and then the next two months were spent doing the actual canning, a brutal job requiring eighteen-hour days under hard, dirty, dangerous conditions. A hundred workers slept in warehouse-like dormitories where they had to douse their mattresses with kerosene to kill the bedbugs. The food was little more than white rice, black beans, and the cheapest type of canned fish. Many fell ill from inadequate nutrition and the brutal work schedule. There were no holidays other than the Fourth of July and no Sundays off. There were no medical facilities, and sometimes men would lose fingers or arms in the machinery. The workers were always dirty, exhausted, and half-starved.

One time Yama was so hungry he broke into the bosses' food supplies and stole enough meat, vegetables, and fruit to hold a sumptuous feast with his fellow workers on the Fourth of July. During that feast, they threw a few cans of overage salmon on the fire to watch them explode and skyrocket in their own Fourth of July fireworks. It was a happy moment of rebellion.

On another occasion, Yama was so exhausted he nearly cried as he worked with a steel-tipped pole to push week-old fish out of bins into the machine known with brutal humor as the "Iron Chink," where the heads and tails and guts were removed. Many of the fish were beginning to rot. The odor nauseated the workers who were exhausted from prying the fish out of the bins for hours at a time. On this day, a top Japanese labor contractor, dressed in a fancy suit, screamed at Yamasaki to work harder. The youth reacted by swinging his steel-tipped pole at the man. Much later, he would recall his action as "insane . . . impulsive." The pole missed, but the boss lost his footing dodging it and fell into a bin full of fish. He came up dripping with salmon blood and slime. The boss couldn't afford to fire Yamasaki; the cannery was too short of workers. The only immediate effect was that Yama lost his ten-dollar bonus for the summer. But his loss of control unnerved Yamasaki as much as or more than it did the boss.

He had some respite from physical labor in the summer of 1932, when his father treated the family to a trip to Japan. Decades later, Yama, who was twenty that summer, wrote of the idyllic time spent horsing around with his cousins and catching catfish in the little stream that cut through his father's family farm. One day, he and two cousins drank a dozen large bottles of beer, with predicable results. "This was my first experience with overdrinking," he wrote later. (That qualifier, "first," hints at Yama's later fondness for, and some difficulty with, alcohol.)

What is extraordinary about Yama's time in the Alaskan canneries is not that a young Japanese American was exploited by brutes in the early Depression years. What is remarkable about Yama's summers in the canneries is how deeply it seared his soul. Decades later in *A Life in Architecture*, Yama would devote almost a quarter of his memoir to these experiences. Though his was a life filled with events and travel and honors, Yama lingered over these summers; clearly these had been central experiences in his life. Most of us forget our summer college jobs the moment we leave them. Yama never forgot his. The mistreatment and exploitation by brutish bosses, and the loss of even the most basic human dignities like clean clothes and beds, drove him to find a better way of life. A young Charles Dickens drew on his months of misery in a blacking factory, where he pasted labels onto pots of boot polish, in his art much later. Yamasaki did the same, using his cannery summers as a spur to create those moments of serenity and delight in architecture that he knew were essential for his heart and mind. "The lessons of those summers," he wrote later, "plus the repugnance I felt for the way we employees were exploited, convinced me that, under such oppression, I could not live with any degree of personal pride, or inspire those whom I was associated with to perform and achieve to their capabilities. This has remained the touchstone by which I have guided my life, my career, and my own office."

NEW YORK YEARS

After graduating from college in the mid-1930s, Yama had to choose between trying to find work locally in Seattle, going to work for his uncle in Tokyo, or striking out on his own in what, even during the Depression, was the center of architecture in America—New York. He went to New York, bearing letters of recommendation from his professors. At first, he carried those letters to firm after firm around Manhattan without success.

Yamasaki grew so skillful at painting watercolors that he taught the art for a time at the university level during his early years in New York. (Image courtesy of Walter P. Reuther Library, Wayne State University)

To earn cash, he wrapped dishes for a Japanese importing firm, later joking about what a good wrapper he made. He took classes at night at New York University both in graduate architecture studies and in watercolor painting. He proved so adept at watercolors that the school invited Yama to teach. For a couple of years in his midtwenties, he taught during the day and worked on his own paintings in the evening.

Eventually, Yama did get the chance to work in the architectural field in New York. At the firm of Githens and Keally, he worked as a draftsman on plans for a new state capitol in Oregon. Yama worked at this job, which paid twice as much as his dish-wrapping gig, for a year, until the project ended and he had to look for work. He then got a job with the firm Shreve, Lamb & Harmon, famed as the architects of the Empire State Building, where he learned all he could about translating architectural drawings into plans that builders could follow to construct or renovate a real building.

The young hopeful who came to New York was a small man—five foot five and about 130 pounds—and well-groomed, invariably dressed neatly in a white shirt and tie with his brown hair neatly combed back. But beneath his unassuming appearance there was an unmistakable intensity. A writer once described Yamasaki as looking "as deceptively serene as a sunning panther." Yama had frequent stomach troubles that, in his auto-biographical writings and interviews, he attributed to the stress and racial discrimination he and other Niseis suffered in America.

Even in his twenties, Yamasaki stood out. His talent, his intelligence, his eagerness and hard work, all paid off quickly even in these lean years. One early boss, Francis Keally, wrote a letter of recommendation for him that glows with future promise: "In addition to his artistic skill, he possesses a keen understanding of the engineering side of construction problems. This combination, as you know, is somewhat rare in our profession. Of all the young men that I have come in contact with during the past ten years, I consider Mr. Yamasaki the most brilliant. In fact, we hope to have the good fortune of having him with us again if and when more work comes our way." And Yama himself, whatever his insecurities, displayed the self-confidence it would take to build his own firm one day. In a 1941 letter to another firm seeking a job, Yama wrote, "My work has brought me into constant contact with almost every phase of the project and this fact, combined with my previous experience, makes me feel fully confident of being able to handle almost any type of work."

Yama met his wife, Teruko, known as Teri, in mid-1941. Like Yama, she was of Japanese descent, and she had come to New York on a scholarship to study piano at the Juilliard School of Music. The couple married after just three months of dating. She was twenty-two and he was twenty-nine. Their decision to marry was made so quickly that Teri didn't have time to shop for a wedding dress; instead she wore her best outfit, a "vivid red gown." They couldn't afford a honeymoon. Yama and Teri lived in a one-bedroom apartment on Manhattan's Upper East Side, which they shared with Yama's brother. Soon Yama's parents moved in, his father having been fired from his longtime job with a shoe store after Pearl Harbor. Fearing his parents would wind up in a West Coast detention center, as so many Japanese Americans did during the war, Yama had urged them to stay with him.

Yama and Teri's marriage date—December 5, 1941—later gave Yama some trouble with a draft board official, who insisted Yama must have known the Japanese were going to attack Pearl Harbor on December 7 and that his marriage must have been one of convenience. Yama already had experienced suspicion and ill treatment due to his heritage, but the war years brought much more. The FBI, navy, and army checked his background thoroughly before he was allowed to work on defense-related jobs. On a New York subway once during the war, a man said to him, "What are you, Chinese or Jap?" When Yama told him it was none of his business, the stranger grabbed Yama by the collar and flashed some sort of badge. "Take your hands off me, I'm an American citizen," Yama told him. The man, perhaps abashed at his own behavior, ran off the train at the next stop. On another occasion, waiting in an air raid shelter during a practice alert, Yama noticed one woman "who stared as if she were trying to burn holes through us." Afterward, the woman ran to a policeman, who apologetically told Yama, "I know you wouldn't be in this public area if you were, but that woman insists that I find out whether or not you're spies." On a third occasion, Yamasaki asked the manager of a new apartment project that he had been working on if he could rent a unit there. The rental manager said no because "your children might get into fights with the other children." Informed that Yama had no kids at that stage, the rental manager still refused.

Such incidents aside, the war years were good to Yamasaki. Instead of serving in the military, he spent the first two years of the war working with the Shreve, Lamb & Harmon firm designing and building the Sampson

Naval Station on the shores of Lake Seneca in upstate New York. It was a big project done on a rush schedule to accommodate the war effort. Yamasaki ran the whole design operation, drawing up the plan for barracks, chapel, garage, and assorted other buildings. He would correct the working drawings his staff made from his designs and then monitor the progress of actual construction. Much later, he called the two years he spent at Sampson perhaps the key learning experience of his career, preparing him to run his own firm one day.

With the Sampson work done, Yama moved to another firm, Harrison, Fouilhoux, and Abramovitz, which had a stronger reputation for design, the more stylish and artistic side of architecture. He enjoyed the work, which was the best paid of his career so far, and he moonlighted teaching drawing at Columbia University. Again his work received glowing reviews. In a February 1944 letter, Columbia offered him a job as an instructor, saying, "We were anxious to retain your services which had been so satisfactory."

Throughout his life, Yama committed his thoughts to paper, creating one autobiographical sketch after another. An undated journal, evidently from his New York years, begins with a simple yet elegant sentence: "Each day, I find a few moments of complete happiness." At another point, he stated his lifelong creed: "For the complexity of modern life, a background of simplicity is almost necessary as balance." The journal could veer into a somewhat purple, impressionistic style, seemingly borrowed from some of the novelists of his day such as Thomas Wolfe, but overall he was a careful, painstaking writer. A letter to the *New York Times* on an important topic might go through repeated drafts before he was satisfied. His *A Life in Architecture* was published late in his life and went through multiple drafts and corrections. Throughout his life, a line of prose or the design of a doorknob could get equal attention. Nothing escaped his eye.

The young Yamasaki also took to political activity, working to help relocate Japanese Americans displaced by the war. In later years, his interest in politics would recede as his architectural practice expanded and his travels ate up much of his time. But at this point his political activity was typical of his abundance of energy and interests.

During his time in New York, where he lived from his midtwenties to his midthirties, Yama worked for several firms and amassed a wealth of practical experience. Occasionally he faced a layoff during the Depression years, but he always left behind a reputation for excellence. When the war ended, he decided to take a position in Detroit with Smith, Hinchman & Grylls as their chief designer, the architect who would take

During World War II, Yama was active in efforts to relocate Japanese Americans away from detention centers on the West Coast. Here he speaks to guests at a dinner in New York about those efforts. Yama's early political activism tended to give way later in his career as the pressures of work grew more intense. (Photo courtesy of the Bancroft Library, University of California-Berkeley)

A charcoal sketch done by Yamasaki during his early New York years for an apartment project, showing Yama's skill as a draftsman and his embrace of modernist design. Note the bold MY initials. (Image courtesy of the Walter P. Reuther Library, Wayne State University)

primary responsibility for major design decisions. SH&G, the city's oldest and usually its largest architectural firm, had been a design powerhouse in the 1920s during Detroit's golden age of building, with its then chief designer Wirt Rowland crafting the look of several classic Detroit skyscrapers including the Penobscot and the Guardian buildings. Following its wartime work, the firm hoped to regain that cachet of fine design. Hiring Minoru Yamasaki, a young, confident New York architect with a growing reputation, was a key step toward that. And so Yamasaki arrived in Detroit in 1945, where he would live for the final half of his life, and where he would craft the designs that would bring him worldwide fame.

GROWING FAME

At SH&G, Yamasaki made his mark quickly.

SH&G got the contract to add a series of new state government buildings near the Michigan state capitol in Lansing. Yamasaki crafted an assemblage of modern office towers. He took care to not block the vistas of the domed capitol itself, and he interspersed plazas among the towers. Although the project was never built as designed, it drew attention in the industry; the magazine *Architectural Forum* called it "a rare combination of efficiency and monumentality in state office buildings." Another early work was his design for a Michigan Bell Telephone building in suburban Birmingham, a few miles north of Detroit. The site was directly across from the town's English-Gothic city hall. Yama, steeped in the nascent modernist movement of the day, bravely gave the building a look that owed a lot to the Bauhaus style, with a flat, mostly unadorned brick facade punctuated by plain windows. Not everyone in the conservative suburb was pleased. In a January 1950 letter, Yama recalled, "When our design appeared in the *Birmingham Eccentric* (the weekly) the citizens really got excited and fourteen of them marched down to the main telephone office in Detroit to protest the hot dog stand architecture."

His most important effort for SH&G was his addition to the US Federal Reserve banking building in downtown Detroit. The older 1920s-era structure, in the neoclassical style, looked like most people's idea of a bank, solid and somber. Yama, an unabashed modernist, gave downtown Detroit its first predominantly glass façade, a steel-frame structure with alternate bands of marble and glass to mark the stories, a thoroughly

Yama as the rising star designer of Smith, Hinchman & Grylls and the model for the state office complex in Lansing, Michigan, that was applauded but never built as planned. (Photo courtesy of the Walter P. Reuther Library, Wayne State University)

modern tower of the sort that leading architects like Ludwig Mies van der Rohe and Gordon Bunshaft were beginning to craft then. More important, Yama set the tower back from the street an extra thirty feet to create space for a small plaza with room for planters. Compared to some of Yama's later plazas, the one at the Federal Reserve is modest. But it showed that even then Yama was thinking about architecture as including what happened outside the building as well as inside; and it pointed the way to the more fully realized examples of the concept that he would create later. The glass and steel facade of the Federal Reserve was a huge success; it nudged design in Detroit forward a generation. The next several major buildings in the city would all follow his lead and utilize a modernist style.

Success did not lessen the pain of discrimination that still dogged Yamasaki and Asian Americans at that time. Making a fairly good salary at SH&G, Yama tried to buy or rent a house in one of the better Detroit suburbs, Birmingham, Bloomfield Hills, or Grosse Pointe. A Realtor he was working with told him it was hopeless, and that the agent would be driven out of the real estate association if he helped Yama buy there. Yama protested the unfairness of it, asking how seemingly even a member of a subversive group could buy with no trouble but not a Nisei. But it was futile to resist. So in 1947, he and Teri and their growing family—they would raise two boys, Taro and Kim, and a daughter, Carol—settled in an 1824 farmhouse on more than seven acres in Troy, a northern suburb, now overrun with development but at the time still mostly rural. They called the farmhouse "Old Willow" after a tree that grew on the property. Many years later, Yama sold the property to land-hungry developers for a huge profit, so perhaps he had the last laugh.

Yama did important work for SH&G but felt handcuffed somewhat by the organizational structure of the large firm, which separated the head designer from the client. "I was never permitted to meet with the client," he said much later. Young, impatient, and ambitious, by 1949 Yama was ready to follow his dream of running his own architectural firm. He left SH&G with two colleagues, George Hullmuth and Joseph Leinweber.

Hellmuth wished to open a branch of Leinweber, Yamasaki, and Hellmuth, based in Detroit, in his hometown of St. Louis. There, Hellmuth's father had connections that led to an astonishingly important commission for the young partners—designing the terminal at the Lambert Airport in St. Louis. Yama crafted a

Yama and Teri with their growing family at the farmhouse in suburban Detroit. (Photo courtesy of the Walter P. Reuther Library, Wayne State University)

composition of structurally pure high-arched concrete domes resting on impossibly narrow points. He gave it a deceptive appearance of egg-shell delicacy that drew widespread praise; that it photographed beautifully added to its appeal.

The St. Louis connection also provided what became, after the World Trade Center, the most difficult commission of Yama's career. Chosen to design a new public housing project in St. Louis, Yamasaki proposed a plan that included a series of low-rise, mid-rise, and high-rise structures, and generous use of trees and communal space. The battles over what became the Pruitt-Igoe complex and how it should be designed were intense and embroiled Yama with both city officials and the public; Yama much preferred low-rise buildings, as he explained in remarks prepared during that time: "Man is a ground animal—it's quite natural for him to live near the earth. The low building with low density is unquestionable more satisfactory than multi-story living. The advantage of living on the ground only a step from the outdoors is a very real one. Nearness to the trees, the flowers and the earth itself offers security that cannot be found from a ten or twelve story window."

But Yama reluctantly saw that high-rises were needed to house the city's growing low-income population on the limited land allotted and still leave room for parks and green space. He hoped to limit the density to no more than thirty-five families per acre, which would have resulted in smaller towers, and he blamed the greed of developers and an inept public housing policy for forcing a density of fifty-five to sixty per acre. The thirty-three-building Pruitt-Igoe complex began to decay from over-crowding and insufficient maintenance almost as soon as it opened in 1956 and was eventually imploded in the 1970s. The entire saga was viewed by the public and by architectural experts alike as a monumental failure of modern architecture to address society's problems. Yama himself called it "one of the sorriest mistakes I ever made in this business. Social ills can't be cured by nice buildings."

One ghastly mistake confirmed Yama's belief that he should trust his own judgment. His firm designed a vast records building in St. Louis for the US Department of Defense to house US Army Corps of Engineers papers. The Corps insisted that the architects omit a sprinkler system because, they said, water would do far more damage to the records than a small fire. Over Yama's protest, the job was built that way; years later, the building burned to the ground and the records were lost.

Yama at Smith, Hinchman & Grylls in the late 1940s with his future partner Joseph Leinweber and their model of a new state office complex in Lansing, Michigan, a project never built as designed. (SmithGroupJJR)

Yamasaki with colleagues and the model for what became the Pruitt-Igoe housing project in St. Louis, which Yama later called the biggest mistake of his career. (Photo courtesy of the Walter P. Reuther Library, Wayne State University)

But there were far more successes than failures for the young firm and its charismatic design chief. Yama and his partners, like any newly launched firm, got mostly smaller jobs at first—a lot of houses, schools, and commercial structures. For commissions like the University Liggett School in suburban Grosse Pointe, Yama designed a series of low-slung modernist buildings of the type known as Miesian—flat-roofed glass-and-steel boxes, buildings connected by covered walkways; it marked a sharp break from the usual style of schools predating this time, heavy with Gothic or other historical details. The buildings he drew often looked light as air, spare yet sufficient, like, as he often said, the stem of a rose—nothing more and nothing less than what is needed to support the flower.

Yamasaki's Japanese ancestry, which up to now had caused him a great deal of pain through discrimination, began to pay off in his favor. In the early 1950s, Americans became fascinated with all things Japanese, with novels like James A. Michener's *Sayonara* and the play and movie *Teahouse of the August Moon* gaining great popularity and introducing a US audience to Japanese themes, albeit viewed through the eyes of American servicemen. Yama already had won renown for himself as the star designer who had pulled Smith, Hinchman & Grylls out of its postwar funk; now he was also the exotic and rather diminutive guru who spoke a new language of art and architecture and who struck many who met him as a genius.

A SEARCH FOR A STYLE

The older architects that Minoru Yamasaki trained with at college and in his New York years were steeped in the Beaux-Arts tradition that prized elaborate historical models from the Renaissance or earlier eras—the sort of architecture that modernists loved to hate. Yamasaki came along late enough in his century to have turned a generational page. "At the time we all disliked the Beaux-Arts system," Yama said many years later. "I suppose because everyone dislikes the thing at hand more than anything else. But, also, because we realized that there was something completely false about the Beaux-Arts."

Early on, Yama took to the modernist idiom. From his New York years, he seems to have gravitated toward what modern architecture could offer, both in aesthetic purity and in its new materials and ways of using them. A charcoal sketch that Yama did for a New York City apartment project in the 1940s demonstrates not only Yama's skill as a draftsman but his acceptance of modernism without any apology. Even the figures of people on the sidewalk in this sketch are something new and different, depicted with just a few curvy lines, enough to signify a head and body and movement. The bold *MY* signature evidences a young man confident in his own vision and abilities.

This early Yamasaki style today looks more reminiscent of the work of the German Bauhaus architects or the work of Mies van der Rohe than the work that later made Yamasaki famous. Indeed, Yama himself later wrote that his earlier buildings were "shallow imitations" of Mies's work. The repeated geometric patterns and surface grilles that distinguish Yama's work at his buildings on Wayne State University's campus are absent in Yama's earlier designs. His Federal Reserve building in downtown Detroit, done in the late 1940s when Yama served as chief designer for Smith, Hinchman & Grylls, is pure glass-and-steel curtain wall, the first of its kind in Detroit. His less-celebrated Michigan Bell Telephone building in suburban Birmingham features an unadorned brick facade broken only by the window openings. Yama's early schools in and around Detroit are beautiful in their simplicity but almost purely functional Miesian boxes.

Henry Guthard was an intern at Smith, Hinchman & Grylls when Yamasaki arrived there in the mid-1940s. He never forgot his early experiences with the new chief designer as Yama crafted the Federal Reserve building: "You know how you remember your early buildings. What Yama wanted for that building, this idea of making this little area of green in the center of this urban compressed area, a little space of serenity and delight, that was the first time that was really done in Detroit. Everything was wall-to-wall concrete. A sea of concrete. I was hanging on every word that Yama had (to say) on that building, and when he eventually left he took me with him, which was just the greatest thing in the world."

But Yamasaki wasn't entirely sold on modern architecture, either, in those early years. "To me, at that time, modern architecture meant battered walls and simple lines," he said much later. He expressed his dislike of the limitations of the glass-box style many times, in interviews and in his writings.

In an article penned by Yamasaki for the November 1955 issue of *Architectural Record*, he lamented the spread of the Lever House style around the country. This modernist glass-box building in midtown

Manhattan, designed by Gordon Bunshaft of Skidmore, Owings and Merrill, had been completed just a few years earlier and already was influencing the design of skyscrapers.

"This portends tragedy," Yamasaki wrote. "As fine as is the original Lever Brothers building, I dread the thought of our cities being endless streets of flush glass, steel and porcelain enamel modules, even beautifully executed." In the same article, he contended that the contemporary modernism, as practiced in the Miesian style, was not the finished and highest manifestation of the style but rather just one stage in a style that was still evolving. "Our aspirations and techniques are too strong to be held back by established thought," he wrote. "The future holds infinity."

The turning point was his 1954 trip around the world. After his recovery from an illness and while working on a commission for a US consulate building in Kobe, Japan, Yama took advantage of his travel there to see the great architecture of both Europe and Asia. A thorough modernist, Yama nonetheless had grown weary of the Miesian contemporary buildings, which he said he had seen "until they came out of my ears." Speaking a few years after his trip, Yama said he had wanted to see the temple houses of Japan, the Taj Mahal in India, the Gothic cathedrals of France, and the Renaissance cities of Italy. "As I looked I got very excited," he said in a 1959 interview: "These older buildings seemed to provide the qualities of experience that were missing in the architecture constructed by our modern society. I felt that one of the most important qualities was the sense of delight and surprise in old cities and buildings. In Rome, for instance, you'd walk through a narrow street and then suddenly you were in an open square. . . . In Japan when you walk into a temple, or even a house, you go from the chaotic activity of the streets to a kind of dream world that is all simple and serene."

He gloried in the cathedrals of Europe, not just in their complex massing but in the play of sunlight and shadow on their facades throughout the day and the striking silhouettes they cast against the sky. In Japan, he found the tranquility he was seeking in the teahouses he entered as he passed from a perfectly proportioned room into a secluded garden where every leaf seemed to have been placed by the hand of God. In India at the Taj Mahal, he understood the magic and power that rigorous design married to a feel for beauty creates for the viewer. He returned from his tour a changed man—and a changed architect.

He even revised his earlier dislike of the classic Beaux-Arts style: "Looking back on it now . . . I'm rather glad that I had this kind of background (in Beaux-Arts) because one of the needs that we are just beginning

McGregor Memorial Conference Center, Wayne State University.
(Photo by Balthazar Korab; courtesy of the Library of Congress)

The Wayne State University College of Education Building, an early example of Yama's use of the Gothic arch for support as well as for its aesthetic qualities. (Photo by John Gallagher)

to understand is the development of feeling for proportion, for refinement and detail. I think that we learned much more about that from the Beaux-Arts than we did from the Bauhaus."

He was in his early forties at this point, the age at which talented architects have often overcome early struggles and have begun to gain the bigger jobs that will cement their reputation. Thanks to his creativity and hard work, and his early luck in getting the high-profile St. Louis jobs, Yama was now in increasing demand, both locally in Detroit and across the country. When Wayne State University beckoned for campus work, Yama began to explore what it meant to bring all of his lessons from Europe, India, and Japan to bear on a problem.

The McGregor Memorial Conference Center provided perhaps his best opportunity. Commissioned just after Yama's return from his travels around the world, the job had plenty of money behind it. The Wayne State leadership, accustomed to purely functional buildings, hardly believed their luck in landing the new star. Functionally, the building is rather simple, with meeting rooms on either side of a central atrium lounge, which is crowned by a skylight running the length of the structure. The richness of the materials used made it something special—teakwood-and-plaster partitions, white marble for the floors and columns, travertine exterior end walls, and folded white slabs of concrete elsewhere. The repeated diamond patterns in the skylight, roofline, and exterior are among Yama's first use of pointed Gothic arches. The Gothic arch was a motif he liked both for its visual appeal and for its structural strength (he would return to it again and again). Henry Guthard, who did the electrical engineering on the McGregor project, said that Yamasaki used the diamond patterns to express the inner tension of the structure being carried through to the exterior for all to see.

But it was in what some might call the secondary spaces that Yama found his true style. He placed the building on a platform to emphasize its importance (another strategy he used repeatedly), and he created an L-shaped pool with three islands for sculpture. Yama had played with the idea of outdoor plazas and seating areas in his earlier buildings, going back as early as his New York years. But at McGregor, for the first time we see the full vision, in which the building itself occupies less than half of the overall footprint of the site.

In other buildings Yama's repeated Gothic arch patterns sometimes seemed repetitive, even tedious, rather than exciting and fresh as they did at McGregor. And sometimes the outdoor plaza, landscaping, and raised platforms for his buildings could overwhelm the nearby street. Even Yama himself would admit that not all his designs worked as well as they should. But by the mid-1950s, he had found his style, and it was his own. It blended Miesian modernism with Japanese subtlety and a feel for sunlight and shadow that he had learned from medieval European masters. Yamasaki took the Miesian glass-box style and softened and humanized it and placed it within an oasis. His designs were not works of sculpture to be admired from afar but places where real people spent a good part of their lives.

His critics later would say that Yama simply put a sort of frilly covering over a basic Miesian glass box. The notion infuriated Yamasaki, who believed that exterior patterns served many purposes. They created a sunlight/shadow effect to give a facade visual interest, and they served a structural purpose, creating an interlocking frame that could carry some of the weight of the building efficiently so that the interiors could remain more open.

Even in the 1960s, when Yama was in his fifties, he was still searching for the perfect blend of form and expression: "The other thing that I have been interested in is that I believe that buildings should have ornament. But I think that the ornament cannot be man-made, rather carved by hand. It can't be handicraft because obviously this is solving nothing. We can't have handicraft ornament on our buildings today. If we do, we are just being somewhat sentimental and proving nothing. But if we can produce really lovely ornaments through the machine, machine-made ornament, we are proving something because then again another element in architecture becomes a part of our technological building."

So ornament plastered to the face of a building wasn't any good. It had to arise from a need. If he chose to apply a screen of some kind to a facade to shut out the sun, it could add ornamental richness and it would do so honestly because it arose from a functional need. Anything added to a building had to be integral to the overall design. "In other words, we can't do the Baroque yet. And I hope we don't," Yama said.

In some of his later buildings, especially in his skyscrapers and other large commissions, he toned down the repeated geometric patterning and expressed the exterior structure more directly, as at the World Trade Center. But even in this later phase of his career, he was creating plazas, landscaping, and sculpture courts as oases of respite for the often-harried office workers he knew would be using his buildings.

Interior of McGregor Memorial Conference Center, Wayne State University.
(Photo by Balthazar Korab; courtesy of the Library of Congress)

24

PERSONAL STRIFE

During the 1950s and '60s—the era of *Mad Men*, of long hours and martini-filled lunches—Yama, putting in brutal hours and overseeing every detail, was prone to burning himself out. "He worked hard and he played hard," says architect Gunnar Birkerts. "He liked company and he liked a good martini. We'd have lunch with a couple of martinis sometimes and we came back and we kept working."

Martini lunches weren't the only problem. Yama suffered a number of serious illnesses over the years, at least some of which could be attributed to the stress he felt from the early discrimination he suffered and the pressure he heaped on himself. The slight Yama was all but consumed with getting every detail of his work absolutely correct. The firm stayed incredibly busy; Yama saw little of his family at this time. By 1954 he underwent surgery for bleeding ulcers, and that was just the start. He would undergo multiple operations for bleeding ulcers and other ills, including one series of four operations in five months during the early 1960s. During his recovery at that time he became "dangerously dependent" for a period on synthetic morphine, from which he slowly weaned himself as he rebuilt his health. In late 1972 he was injured in an auto accident and took several weeks to recover.

After he recovered from his 1954 illness, he decided to split from the St. Louis half of the firm, establishing Minoru Yamasaki & Associates. His goal now would be to run a firm of no more than about fifty people, including architects, engineers, and model makers. Any bigger than that, he determined, and he would not be able to concentrate on the high-quality designs that he was committed to turning out. But the illnesses would reoccur. In 1963, he was back in the hospital and, for a time, not expected to live. He recovered and returned to work.

His devotion to his work, and perhaps his inner turmoil, took a toll on Yama's marriage, too. He and Teri divorced in 1961. Two short-lived marriages followed, along with a relationship with a nurse Yama met during one of his hospital stays. "I was a bad boy," he told a reporter later. Teri put it this way: "A celebrated man must be superhuman to withstand the tremendous adulation." Yama's friend and neighbor, the celebrated photographer Balthazar Korab, put it more bluntly: "Now Yama is big enough that he could get everything he could not get before." He and Teri stayed in contact during the years following their divorce, usually through their children's activities, and they finally reunited and remarried in 1969, spending the rest of Yama's life

Yamasaki traveled the world both for work and for pleasure. (Photo courtesy of the Walter P. Reuther Library, Wayne State University)

Yamasaki's smile belied his often-troubled life. (Photo courtesy of the Walter P. Reuther Library, Wayne State University)

Yamasaki with Teri. (Photo courtesy of the Walter P. Reuther Library, Wayne State University)

together. At the time of their remarriage, Teri would say, "I will try to be more of a Japanese wife." Yama's take on it: "I'm just going to be nicer to her." Teri told a reporter at the time of their remarriage that Yama had mellowed; he could now talk about something other than his work, and he had become a gourmet from dining in the top restaurants around the world.

WORKING IN YAMA'S OFFICE

No architect does it alone. Every architect relies on engineers, designers, draftsmen, project managers, landscape architects, and others to carry his vision. Yamasaki was no different. But there was never any doubt who ran the office or whose vision was paramount. "He ran that whole office with what I would call a compassionate iron hand," Kip Serota, a longtime designer in the office, said. He continued:

> Someone actually had to put it on paper, but you had Yama looking over your shoulder *all the time.* There wasn't anything that got past him. And as near as I could make out, if you didn't have that kind of relationship with him, those people would move on to some other organization. You always had architects in there that wanted to do it their way, and I used to always say if you want do it your own way, then you should have your own office. This is Yamasaki's office. And if you don't know where he's going philosophically, you probably shouldn't be here.

Gunnar Birkerts, who worked for Eero Saarinen before spending a few years with Yamasaki and then starting his own celebrated firm, contrasted his two mentors. Eero Saarinen, he said, kept "pounding and pounding and pounding" a design idea until he had it right, often doing that in tandem with his team of designers. "Yama came up with the idea internally," Birkerts said. "He just sprung up at the table and said, 'I've got it! I've got it!'" Of these two modes of creation—Saarinen's "beating it long enough to get the best solution" and Yama's more intuitive approach—Birkerts preferred Yamasaki's way. "He was an architect like I imagined an architect was," he said.

Birkerts worked with Yama on the Education building at Wayne State and later on an airport in Saudi Arabia. "He was, to me, truly an architect who worked with emotion, with talent, and with intuition, and

Yama's team at work in his studio in Troy. (State Archives of Michigan)

[those are] of course the categories I consider important in architecture." Birkerts added, "He was a perfectionist. He never did a building that wasn't worth all his attention."

"Yama's presence was ubiquitous," Henry Guthard recalled from the distance of many years:

> He was everywhere, everywhere you go Yama would be talking to a mechanical engineer, talking about the size of the grilles that (cover) the refrigeration machinery, and can the grilles be turned a certain way, and can the railing of the grilles be finer, thicker, thinner, can it be reduced, placed in a different location, can it be invisible from the street. Then 10 minutes later he's in the electrical department with the lighting person talking about how to illuminate the space. Yama in his very patient way would listen to that and give the person great credit for his knowledge and their wisdom but then just suggest maybe some little improvement, little change, what do you think of that, totally different concept for the one that was being designed by the lighting engineer the way they'd been doing it for the last 20 years. And the net result would be that Yama would get a totally different lighting system, the one that he wanted, and the person doing it would get full credit for coming up with this composite.

Not every professional would thrive under this regime. Yama recalled in his memoir the time an important client was coming to visit the firm and Yama told everyone to help him tidy up the office. Yama was pushing a broom when he noticed a young man, recently hired, sitting on his stool in a corner. When Yama asked why he wasn't helping, the man answered, "I was hired to be an architect, not a janitor." Yama fired him on the spot.

John Suhr, an architect who worked for Yama for a few years in the 1970s, recalled how he had been fired by Yama when he learned that Suhr had slipped a design concept into a project against Yama's wishes. Some people found Yama egotistical or abrupt, but for those who connected with Yama and his vision, a career at the firm could be exciting and fulfilling. According to Henry Guthard:

> He was everywhere. He had such energy. Much of his energy was a desire to have all the parts of the building work right. It wasn't just the architecture. All the parts. He'd come and ask me some question about lighting, and he would make me think that I was giving him an answer that really

contributed to the building. He was the first one I ever really saw that made everyone feel he was part of the team. He gave the feeling that he was looking right at you, and he would say, all of you are the designers. He would have been one of the best football coaches in the world!

Yama often revealed his fascination with the structure of nature, as in his oft-repeated example of the stem of a rose that supported the flower with nothing more and nothing less than was necessary. "I've heard him say that so many times," Guthard said. "I can see him gesturing with his hands about how you bring the structure into the building. And of course as a young guy I'm sitting there thinking 'God, that's wonderful.'"

Certainly Yama drove himself harder than anyone in his office. His frequent illnesses, multiple operations, and a troubled marital history testified to that. He was on the road for work-related travels for one-third to one-half of the year in his peak years. And every detail of a project had to be correct, perfect.

Yama's insistence on perfection from himself and everyone else led to one aspect of Yama's routine that became his trademark—the model-making that his office became known for. Guthard surmises that Yamasaki's insecurity led him to doubt the utility of flat two-dimensional drawings of a building. Yama needed to see the way sunlight would play across the facade and what shadows it would cast at each time of day. So he had created a model shop in the office that made models for each project—sometimes dozens of models for each concept—with laser-cut detailing that few if any other architects were doing in the 1950s and '60s. Instead of showing the building in isolation, Yama would create extensive tabletop models of entire downtowns to show how the building would fit in. Yama had a moveable camera on a rig that could travel around a model and through it so that he could see it from the inside out.

"The doors, the hinges, doorknobs, the sound of the mechanical equipment, the regularity of the functional systems, all of those things were important to him," Guthard said.

Yama could lighten the intensity in his office at times with a pawky show of humor when the occasion called for it. Henry Guthard tells one such story: "Once there was a guy who was very critical of a project, not a bad guy, but he was slowing the project down a little bit. So Yama had a three-dimensional model built and

Yama with his model for Wayne State's College of Education.
(Photo courtesy of the Walter P. Reuther Library, Wayne State University)

photographed, and they inserted photos of this guy smiling inside the building, and when they presented it, the guy thought he was Rip van Winkle just waking up from somewhere."

Yama's sense of humor also came into play when he was designing the Michigan Consolidated Gas Company headquarters at One Woodward Avenue in Detroit. As Yama himself tells it:

> The company's slogan, "Gas is Best," is prominently displayed on their tanks and various service buildings throughout the city. At every preliminary meeting, one of the company representatives was sure to ask where the sign bearing the slogan was to be placed on the new building. I would always shudder inwardly and avoid the question. When the basic design was completed, we prepared a rather impressive, large-scale model of the building, complete with internal lighting. We also prepared a "little white box" with cutout letters, batteries, and lamps that I carried in my shirt pocket, a concealed wire leading to a switch in my trousers pocket. In the course of the presentation, we turned out the room lights and illuminated the model; predictably, the same old question about the sign came up. I flicked the switch, and "Gas is Best" blazed across my chest. When the laughter subsided, I explained that I would prefer to put the sign on myself, rather than on the building, so we have no sign on the building, and (company president) Ralph McElvenny has a souvenir miniature sign-box, batteries, wires, and all.

YAMA'S USE OF MATERIALS

To bring to life an architectural vision that begins in the heart and mind, an architect needs to understand materials. And here is where Yamasaki excelled.

Materials may come straight from the earth (wood, stone), or be handcrafted (brick, adobe, primitive glass), or they may roll off modern production lines (steel, enamel, aluminum, porcelain, the latest energy-saving glass composites). Architects learn in school and in practice the basics of how these products work—the bearing strength of steel, or how to fasten an aluminum panel to a wall. But the best architects go beyond the basics. Certainly Yama strove mightily to master the materials in his arsenal.

By his round-the-world voyage in 1954, Yama sensed the limitations of the International glass-box style of architecture that so dominated his profession. Besides the often chilly nature of these machine-like buildings, there was another aspect that bothered Yama. As he discussed in a 1959 interview, reliance on these factory-made materials put the *manufacturer* in complete control of the finished product. As Yama put it: "The manufacturer produces so many yards of porcelain, enamel, or aluminum extrusions, or glass of a particular shape, and since it's less costly to buy in stock, then the tendency is to build buildings of this kind. So what happens is that our total environment then becomes a slave to the machine."

Seeking control over his finished buildings, Yama sought products that had a plasticity that he could shape to his liking. After searching, he chose a product both ancient and modern—concrete.

Concrete—the product of mixing cement and other elements—is as old as the Romans, who learned to mix sand, ash, or other materials with water and a binding agent to create a mixture that, when allowed to set, was solid and strong yet capable of being molded. The Romans fashioned their famed Coliseum from concrete, and the dome of the Pantheon is the largest non-reinforced concrete dome in the world. Modern manufacturers refined the concept into what they called "precast," in which the materials are poured when wet into a form or mold that in theory can take any shape the architect likes. As Yama said in his 1959 interview: "It's very important for the architect in a society to be able to express himself because responsible architects then will try to produce a lovely environment for man. And this is the reason why I like precast concrete. I believe that precast concrete is a means by which architectural expression can again become a valid and important part of the activity of man."

Henry Guthard cites the Education building at Wayne State University as the precursor for Yama's use of precast as his material of choice, particularly for high-rise buildings. Of critical importance to precast is the aggregate that is mixed in—tiny bits of stone meant to adhere to the surface to give sparkle and character to an otherwise flat surface. Yama chose white polar quartz and Botticino marble for his aggregate, and then went on to learn everything he could about how those materials worked in practice.

Probing the nature of aggregate with a man from the American Precast Co., Yama learned that white polar quartz would come in a crystalline form with a series of surfaces that were relatively flat. He learned that the flat surfaces of the tiny bits of stone meant rain and dust would stay on the surfaces a bit longer than if the tiny bits of stone were less angular. The longer the rain and dust perched there, the more calcification would occur and, over time, the stone would no longer sparkle. "Yama came out knowing everything there was to know about precast," Guthard said.

Yama's solution to the calcification issue: He had suppliers tumble the aggregate so that the angular edges were softened and rounded off. That allowed the rain and dust to slide off more quickly, which kept the building looking cleaner longer. "This type of technology was just not considered" until then, Guthard said, adding, "Was he interested in materials? Oh, man, he sure as hell was."

PUTTING IT ALL TOGETHER

When he returned from his 1954 world tour, Yama's goal was to infuse some of the serenity and delight of Japanese temples as well as the play of sunshine and shadow he found in older cities in Europe into his own designs while staying true to the technology and means of his time.

Two commissions in the mid-1950s provided him the canvas he needed. Both the McGregor Memorial Conference Center, as discussed earlier, on the campus of Wayne State University in Detroit and the Reynolds Metals building in Southfield, Michigan, emerged from his drawing board with complex facades that softened and humanized the Miesian glass box. Both contained the elaborate water features and gardens that, to Yama, were as important to the overall site as the structure itself. Both projects became award winners and drew attention to the young architectural firm and its leader.

Yama's first high-rise structure, often called a precursor to the World Trade Center, was a new headquarters for the Michigan Consolidated Gas Company in downtown Detroit that opened in 1963. The thirty-story tower, now known as One Woodward, included a delicate grillwork of white precast concrete covering what other architects might have made a simple glass curtain wall; the water feature and landscaping at the base provided that oasis of serenity that was so important to the architect.

Yama's design for the US Science Pavilion at the Seattle World's Fair of 1962 would earn him national attention. To mark the entrance, Yama designed five one-hundred-foot-tall arched towers, which appeared as

Yamasaki's Science Pavilion for the Seattle World's Fair in the early 1960s made the cover of *Time* magazine and helped earn him the commission to design the World Trade Center. (Photo by Balthazar Korab courtesy of the Library of Congress)

gossamer as spider webs against the sky. *Time* magazine put Yamasaki on its cover in January 1963 with the Science Pavilion in the background.

The Science Pavilion led to a profound development in Yama's career. The ethereal Asian American architect who had earned a modest reputation within his profession was about to become world famous.

THE WORLD TRADE CENTER

If there is a supreme irony in the life of Minoru Yamasaki, it's this: an architect who struggled his entire career to celebrate the serene, the peaceful, and the humane is best remembered today for the most gargantuan project of his day, twin towers destroyed in a most horrific act of terrorism. The World Trade Center project was the pivotal point of Yama's career. It transformed him from an architect of modest projects like schools and university buildings into an architect of skyscrapers. It forced him to fit his notions of human-scale design to the ambitions of overreaching real estate developers in the most overbuilt environment on earth. The World Trade Center shattered the bond that had been growing between Yama and many of his admirers, including the notable architecture critic Ada Louise Huxtable of the *New York Times*, who switched from a strong supporter of Yama to one of his harshest critics. The project consumed ten years and more of Yama's life and energies, and the critical drubbing the project took wounded Yama deeply.

It began with a moment of low comedy. One day in 1962, when Yama was nearing his fiftieth birthday and at the height of his creative powers, he received a letter in his office from the Port Authority of New York and New Jersey. The letter inquired if Yamasaki wished to apply to design a new $280,000,000 project to house international trade functions in lower Manhattan. Yama called his staff together to point out the obvious typographical error in the letter, the addition of an extra zero to the dollar amount. That sort of carelessness, he cautioned, could cast an entire office in a bad light.

But the amount was correct, and when Yama learned of the true scope of this project he told the Port Authority leadership his firm was too small to handle it. The Port Authority leaders disagreed, urging Yama to take the invitation seriously. In fact, they had had Yamasaki's work on their radar for some time.

His growing fame landed Yama on the cover of *Time* magazine in January 1963, a few months after the World Trade Center commission was announced. (Photo of *Time* cover by John Gallagher)

A top Port Authority staffer, Guy Tozzoli, had visited the Seattle World's Fair some months earlier to scope out ideas for the planned New York World's Fair of 1964. Tozzoli was stunned by Yama's work for the Science Pavilion. Set on a raised base, Yama's design was a U-shaped collection of buildings clustered around a plaza in which Yama's five arched towers rose, as graceful as flowers against the sky. The assemblage struck Tozzoli as ethereal, otherworldly, and beautiful. In the midst of a busy world's fair, Yamasaki's plaza and towers created an oasis of serenity and delight. At the Port Authority's insistent urging, Yama overcame his own doubts. His selection as the architect of the World Trade Center project was announced in September 1962.

He began his new task by walking the streets of Manhattan, where he had walked so many years before as a young trainee architect. Back in those early years, when he was working on Forty-Fourth Street in New York, he used to stroll to Rockefeller Center on nice days and wander through the gardens, observing how the visitors and workers enjoyed the oasis nestled among the very tall buildings. The lesson he took away was that "it doesn't really matter in Manhattan how high you go up; what really counts to the people using buildings is their scale at or near the ground." The real opportunity at the Trade Center, he felt, was to create a "great outdoor space, shielded from vehicular traffic, easily accessible to pedestrians, and a pleasure to the occupants." That vision would require razing multiple blocks of older structures in lower Manhattan for what would become the 16-acre Trade Center; but as Yama walked the site he came to feel that would be no great tragedy. "I thought it was very fortunate that there was not a single building worth saving in the fourteen-block site," he wrote much later. All the businesses there—bars, clothing stores, radio and electronic shops, all in older buildings—could be relocated without much loss. And the opportunity it would open up to create something special was worth the cost.

Yama balked at first at the Port Authority's insistence that the project produce the tallest buildings in the world. He knew from the start about the Brobdingnagian space demands of the Port Authority—ten million square feet of office space—but he thought at first he might satisfy that with a series of smaller buildings grouped around a central plaza. But the Port Authority made clear, in multiple meetings and communications that to this day echo with a whiff of megalomania, that the buildings would be the tallest

This is the image of Yamasaki released by the Port Authority of New York and New Jersey upon Yama's selection as architect for the World Trade Center. (Photo courtesy of the Walter P. Reuther Library, Wayne State University)

on the planet. Yama protested that they would remain the tallest only for a short time at best; even then, the taller Sears Tower in Chicago was in development. But there was no resisting the client's wishes. So the Twin Towers grew taller and stouter on Yama's design table, until they became the outsized monoliths derided by critics later on.

Yama's model makers went to work and created models ten feet tall, bigger than any they had produced before, so big that at one point the ceiling panels of the office had to be removed to fit them in the studio. When the first design images were released to the press, Ada Louise Huxtable of the *New York Times* praised them. In a column published on February 2, 1964, she hailed the design as "an outstandingly serious and searching attempt to put together a supercolossal complex on a superior level of structural and esthetic design." She called Yama "a first-rate talent" who, collaborating with New York-based technical consultant Emery Roth, had produced "a first-rate design." Such praise from a critic Yama admired must have eased any doubts he had. But Huxtable would not remain in Yama's corner.

What struck Yama as unfair later, when the criticism turned what he called "violently emotional," was that nobody seemed to appreciate the ingenious engineering solutions he and his team had crafted. There were several absolutely daunting challenges from the beginning. One was how to anchor the buildings to Manhattan's bedrock. The Port Authority's suggested solution was to dig down through the ground about thirty-five feet and then send down the steel shafts to bedrock at seventy feet below the surface. But that method was prone to flooding from the waters of nearby New York Harbor. Indeed, the water pressure pressing in at the bottom of the excavation would exert enormous stress. Better and sturdier, Yama said, to excavate the entire enormous site all the way to bedrock and somehow find a way to keep the waters of New York Harbor from bursting through and flooding the hole. The solution, discovered by a Port Authority engineer named Martin Kapp, who had seen it in a subway under construction in Milan, was called a "slurry wall." In this method, narrow holes were dug all the way to bedrock then filled with slurry—a mixture of clay and water that was dense enough to hold back the water pressure. A steel cage was forced down and concrete injected into it; and since the concrete was heavier than slurry, the slurry rose to the surface, where it was drained away, leaving a three-foot-thick reinforced concrete wall section anchored to the bedrock. This was repeated multiple times

The World Trade Center models were the biggest that Yama's celebrated model shop ever produced.
(Photo by Balthazar Korab; courtesy of the Library of Congress)

around the entire perimeter, until the entire below-ground hole had been secured by its concrete shell. Workers could walk dry-shod across the entire floor.

Yama was equally proud of the wind-bracing system devised for the two towers. High winds at the upper levels of very tall buildings can cause skyscrapers to sway like the tops of trees; there were tales of water sloshing out of toilets and other unpleasantness. So architects over the years had learned to lessen that tendency to sway in a variety of ways. Older towers like the Empire State Building carried so much stone on their exteriors that the sheer weight stabilized the structure. But modern glass-box towers were lighter and therefore more prone to sway. Many architects designed elaborate cross-bracing in the core of a tower, but Yama wanted to keep the interior of the World Trade Center uncluttered and rentable. So he settled on a structural truss system on the exterior; what many later criticized as a lacy applique on the exterior was actually an impressive network of vertical and horizontal structural members that carried the load with grace and efficiency. Indeed, one reason why the Twin Towers stood as long as they did on September 11, 2001, was that the exterior structural system transferred the weight from the damaged portion of the exterior to still-sound portions.

And innovation came to bear on the design of the elevators' cores as well, which in a very tall structure could take up a significant amount of space, decreasing the amount of rentable floor space that developers demanded. So Yama and his team designed three vertical zones in each tower. High-speed express cabs would carry passengers to the upper zones, where they would change to a "local" elevator to reach their floors. Yama estimated the system provided 15 to 17 percent more rentable floor space, an innovation worth millions of dollars in rents to the Port Authority.

The look of the exterior evolved in the design studio over time, with Yama scaling back some of his earlier geometric patterns in favor of an unbroken line of narrow window frames that were meant to carry a gaze all the way to the sky. Henry Guthard recalls that Yama had to argue with the Port Authority over the depth of the window frames on the exterior, with Yama seeking a few inches greater depth to create more sunlight and shadow effects on the exterior. The grand plaza at the base measured five acres—nearly a third of the entire site—and was dominated by Fritz Koenig's twenty-five-foot-tall bronze spherical sculpture.

Yamasaki looking pleased with the World Trade Center models in the background.
(Photo courtesy of the Walter P. Reuther Library, Wayne State University)

Yama had convinced himself that the prodigious size of his towers would not burden the skyline. "It is only the first-time visitor who cranes his neck to see the tops of higher buildings," he wrote later. When his staff expressed doubts, he had them walk around the Empire State Building a few times, as Yama himself had at the start of the project. "They came back convinced, as I was, that there was no diminution of the soul, no antlike feelings in the face of such a large object. Man had made it and could comprehend it, and its parts could be understood to relate to its whole." Nonetheless, Yama seems to have misjudged the impact that these oversized gleaming white boxes would have on New York's famous skyline. To many viewers, they seemed badly out of proportion with the city, but Yama never doubted what he had done.

Others did, and said so in ways that were cutting and cruel: "Manhattan's Tower of Babel," and "The World's Tallest Fiasco," to cite two headlines upon the project's 1973 opening. Perhaps the deepest insult came from former supporter Ada Louise Huxtable, who lampooned the Trade Center towers in her 1973 column for the *New York Times.* Headlined "Big but Not So Bold: Trade Center Towers are Tallest but Architecture Is Smaller Scale," the column brutalized Yama's work: "The towers are pure technology, the lobbies are pure schmaltz and the impact on New York of two 110-story buildings . . . is pure speculation." She called Yama's delicate Gothic-inspired branches at the lower level "a detail that does not express structure so much as tart it up," adding, "the Port Authority has built the ultimate Disneyland fairytale blockbuster. It is General Motors Gothic."

Within days, Yama sent Huxtable an eight-page single-spaced rebuttal. He worked hard on it, going through four drafts before he had it right. He began by citing his favorite quote from Ralph Waldo Emerson: "The line of beauty is the result of perfect economy. The cell of the beehive is built at that angle which gives the most strength with the least wax. The bone or the quill of the bird gives the most alar strength with the least weight." He thus began his explanation of the structural innovations at the Trade Center, citing the exterior framing that held up the massive structure allowing for column-free interior space. He justified his narrow windows, barely a shoulder-span wide, as both energy saving and less likely to induce a fear of heights among the tenants; acrophobia was something that Yama himself famously suffered from. He pointed out that the towers were built at a relative bargain price thanks to all the innovative engineering, and he defended his plaza at the base as a place in which office workers, often harried, could find some

Famous due to the World Trade Center commission, Yamasaki meets President Lyndon Baines Johnson.
(Photo courtesy of the Walter P. Reuther Library, Wayne State University)

peace and serenity. Much later, in his autobiography, Yama mused that much of the criticism of the towers revealed an anti-urban prejudice of those not willing to accept the density and diversity of Manhattan. In a 1978 article in *Smithsonian* magazine, Yama explained his motives in creating the plaza for the trade center's workers: "What I wanted to do was to give them a paved garden, like San Marco, where they can spend a little time away from traffic, a place totally for pedestrians. Some of them have to get away from the tension of their jobs, some from the monotony."

It did no good. Like concrete, the critical judgment on the World Trade Center had set in place. For every fan and defender of the World Trade Center architecture, there seemed to be two or three critics, and the critics were more vociferous. Yama would design many more buildings in the final ten years of his life, working all over the world, the commissions flowing in, his creativity undimmed, but the World Trade Center inevitably would become the first line of his obituary.

YAMA AND THE CRITICAL WARS

Even moderately famous architects often find themselves embroiled in the intense creative debates of their day. Of all the artistic clashes that roiled the twentieth century, perhaps none was so intense as the conflict dividing architects at midcentury.

Within this world, modernists of the International style championed by Ludwig Mies van der Rohe were battling not only the historical styles of past centuries but the New Formalists, architects who adapted classical forms to modern demands, including exterior columns, white or light-colored stone, and symmetrical facades. Among these New Formalists were Minoru Yamasaki, Edward Durrell Stone, and Morris Lapidus. In a 1972 column in the *New York Times*, Ada Louise Huxtable criticized Yamasaki: "As another master, Mies van der Rohe, wisely said, 'You don't invent a new architecture every Monday morning,' although a lot of architects keep trying. Current campus construction is full of acrobatic novelties and vacuous vulgarities, such as Princeton's own Woodrow Wilson School of Public Affairs by Minoru Yamasaki."

This was mild criticism compared to what some in the East Coast architectural establishment were dishing out. Vincent Scully, the grand man of architectural criticism and history at Yale, dismissed Yama's

World Trade Center, New York, NY. (Photo by Balthazar Korab; courtesy of the Library of Congress)

masterpiece, the McGregor Memorial Conference Center, as a "twittering aviary." Fellow modernist Gordon Bunshaft remarked, "Yamasaki's as much an architect as I am Napoleon. He was an architect, but now he's nothing but a decorator." Another contemporary, I. M. Pei, flicked away Yama's Federal Science Pavilion in Seattle as a "mere artistic caprice." When Yama died in 1986, the noted architectural critic Paul Goldberger told the press, "He did a number of very prominent buildings, even if they didn't change the course of architecture. What he tended to do was take modern buildings and sort of cover them with frilly decorations, which he saw as an antidote to the coldness of the glass box."

What had bothered these critics so much? Eric Hill, now a professor of architecture at the University of Michigan, coauthor (with this author) of *AIA Detroit: The American Institute of Architects Guide to Detroit Architecture,* and project director of the State of Michigan's Michigan Modern project, studied architecture in Boston in the late 1960s and early '70s. Hill recalls that Yamasaki, Stone, and other New Formalists were not perceived by the academic world as top-tier innovators, or what the public today calls "starchitects." Yama and Stone were thought to be dealing mostly with cosmetics, with the "wallpaper" of the exterior, rather than introducing any spatial innovations, like the curves and swoops that Eero Saarinen played with in his TWA Terminal in New York. Yama was viewed as one step above Morris Lapidus, the neo-baroque architect famed (or condemned) for crafting the Fontainebleau resort in Florida. Lapidus's brand of design would be dismissed as the Disneyfication of architecture. The New Formalism was viewed as little more than putting a pretty face on the same old spatial plan. "Very decorative," Hill recalls, adding, "Ornament was still a crime." Of course Yama's work was far from that of another of the reigning champions, Paul Rudolph, whose Brutalist-style Boston city hall was then just being completed.

The critical reception was hardly all negative. Quite the opposite; the Yamasaki papers in the Reuther Library at Wayne State University are stuffed with citations and awards and commendations and honorary degrees, with invitations to lecture at Harvard and Yale, to serve as a jury member for this or that competition. There are numerous clippings of articles praising a Yama design, congratulatory missives from fellow architects. A letter from the architect Philip Johnson in particular must have pleased Yama. Johnson noted that he had seen a display of design proposals for a US embassy project, a commission that went to Yama's

Yamasaki in his office at the height of his fame. (Photo courtesy of the Walter P. Reuther Library, Wayne State University)

Yama's design for an airport in Saudi Arabia proved so popular that the nation put the image on its currency.
(Photo courtesy of the Walter P. Reuther Library, Wayne State University)

friend Eero Saarinen; Johnson said he had found Yama's proposal the best of them all, even if it didn't win. And the new jobs flowed in nonstop. By the mid- to late 1950s, Yama was so successful that had to reject numerous invitations to appear somewhere to speak or to jury a competition, citing the overwhelming press of work in his office.

Eric Hill came to Detroit in the 1980s and worked for a variety of firms, and only then did he begin to see in Yamasaki's work what the establishment had missed. Perhaps to appreciate a Yamasaki building it was necessary to see it in its setting, complete with its plaza, garden, and water feature, and to see how what appeared to be a decorative facade—what Goldberger and other critics dismissed as frilly decorations—was part of a carefully conceived structural plan that added to the aesthetic appeal of a building as well as to its structural strength. "I had not known about McGregor," Hill said in a 2014 interview. "McGregor was a masterpiece. The whole thing works. Michigan Gas on first look looked like so many other of his buildings but on second look it's far more significant, far deeper. So I began to really appreciate his work by seeing it, by experiencing it."

THE LATER YEARS

If the World Trade Center commission brought Yama as much pain as pleasure, it also ensured his worldwide fame. By the 1970s, commissions were flowing in from around the world. Developers of skyscrapers called on him, and Yama crafted a series of tall buildings in major downtowns: One M&T Plaza in Buffalo (completed in 1966); the Montgomery in Chicago (1972); Century Plaza Towers in Los Angeles (1975); Federal Reserve Bank of Richmond (1975); Rainier Tower in Seattle (1977); 100 Washington Square in Minneapolis (1981); and Torre Picasso in Madrid, Spain, completed in 1988, after Yama's death. These later towers included some of his trademarks, the plaza at the base and the gleaming white exteriors, although the overall impression is that these lack some of the inventiveness and freshness of Yama's earlier more modest work. Yama had struggled against poverty and discrimination in his youth; perhaps in his mature years he found the lure of doing the biggest and most prestigious projects too much to resist. Perhaps he felt he had already solved the puzzle of the smaller, more modest project, and wished to explore the design of buildings that reached for the sky. Or maybe he just enjoyed the fame that skyscraper design brought him.

The living room of the Yamasaki residence in Bloomfield Township, Michigan. (Photo by Balthazar Korab; courtesy of the Library of Congress)

A courtyard at the Yamasaki residence in Bloomfield Township, Michigan. (Photo by Balthazar Korab; courtesy of the Library of Congress)

Office skyscrapers weren't the only work. In the 1970s and '80s, Yama's office turned out designs for the Tulsa Performing Arts Center, the Saudi Arabian Monetary Agency in Riyadh, the Miyako Hotel in Tokyo, the Shiga Sacred Garden Temple in Japan, and many others. Not everything designed got built, of course, as any architect knows. There was a new town plan for Lagos, Nigeria, that was expected to keep the office busy for years, but the client had to flee for his life in a military coup in 1974, and the project was shelved.

But even in this later stage of Yama's career, he was working in Southeast Michigan. His design for Temple Beth El in suburban Birmingham, built in 1974, evoked in its structure a tent the Israelites might have used when wandering in the desert after fleeing Egypt; and the temple's interior brilliantly allowed for expanded seating during high holy days as well as glimpses out to the landscaped grounds that remained key to Yama's vision. In a brochure written for the dedication, Yama, no strong believer in formal religion, expressed his own lifelong creed: "In order to believe in God, man must first believe in himself. He cannot do this unless he is given dignity by his surroundings."

In the late 1960s and early '70s, he also built two "self-portraits"—a new office building for his firm on Big Beaver Road in Troy and a new residence for himself and Teri in a wooded glade in Bloomfield Township. Both of these buildings evoked a Japanese simplicity and serenity. They ranked high among Yama's most satisfying works.

In his last years, Yamasaki worked hard on his memoir, *A Life in Architecture*, going through multiple drafts that he painstakingly corrected. He remained active to the end. Worn out by a lifetime of labor, Yama died of cancer in 1986 at the age of seventy-three.

LEGACY

In *A Life in Architecture*, Yama estimated that his office had designed more than 250 buildings. Many we would judge today to be outstanding, others merely functional, and a few were, as Yama admitted, "just plain bad." The mere total, impressive though it may be, doesn't adequately define Yamasaki's impact on daily life. Through his never-ceasing exploration of form and expression, he struggled to give each client something beyond the basic requirement of space wrapped up in a pretty package. He continued to seek the very best

Yama in a more tranquil moment. (Photo courtesy of the Walter P. Reuther Library, Wayne State University)

from himself and his team in all matters—the best structural solution to the problem, the best materials, and the utmost that could be achieved in every detail. And even beyond that quest, he sought to infuse some measure of that serenity and delight that he found in nature and in places like the Taj Mahal and Japanese tea gardens. He burdened himself with that lofty goal early in life and never gave up working toward it. As Gunnar Birkerts has said, Yamasaki was an architect the way we imagine an architect to be.

Yama's critics, who accused him of simply wallpapering a glass box with a frilly screen, missed the mark by a wide margin. With his realization that the entire site of a building was part of the architecture, he made room for those plazas, gardens, pools, fountains, and other details that have become part of any important building today, although seldom done as well as Yama did them at, say, the McGregor Memorial Conference Center. Most architects labor over meeting the client's requirements for how the space will work in practice, but Yama's insights went beyond that, into thinking about how real people would react to a space in their day-to-day lives. He felt that most people struggled to find a little peace and tranquility, and he made it his mission to give it to them. As Henry Guthard says, "Yama always taught us to separate to the maximum extent possible space between the edge of the property and the building, so that there would be something soft and green. And if indeed this becomes a small oasis in a canyon of buildings, it will be what it is and it'll never change. It will always have that value."

Yama seemed to achieve his goals more often in his smaller buildings than in skyscrapers. The colossal scale of the World Trade Center overwhelmed the New York skyline, and his many other skyscrapers, though more in proportion to their surroundings, do not satisfy quite like Temple Beth El's breathtaking interior or the clean fresh lines of the Federal Reserve in Detroit. And Yama's most modest projects—his own residence, his office in Troy, the McGregor center, and many others—show Yama at his very best.

Interestingly, the term applied to his work, New Formalism, works with only some of his buildings, usually the biggest projects like his skyscrapers. Look at some of Yama's earlier schools, residences, and religious buildings, and you see a designer more in tune with one of his idols, Mies van der Rohe, than with other New Formalists. While his work is thoroughly modernist, it remains uniquely his own. He explored a range of expressive styles and forms through his career.

We often think of architecture as the most solid and permanent of art forms, but this is not always so. Some of Yama's buildings already have been lost, including the fine little office building he designed for his firm in Troy and, of course, the World Trade Center towers in New York. Other Yama buildings have suffered the debilitating erosion of time and neglect. But sometimes fortune smiles on architecture. In 2013, Wayne State University completed its restoration of the pools at the McGregor Memorial Conference Center in Detroit, which in any ranking of Yama's works would find a place at or near the very top. The restoration gave back to the community Yama's original vision for McGregor, a place of tranquility amid a bustling city. McGregor today serves as a meeting space for people of diverse cultures and backgrounds; that it plays its role so well remains a tribute to its creator. Minoru Yamasaki proved again and again that the humanistic values of serenity and delight never go out of style.

SELECTED PROJECTS

MICHIGAN BELL TELEPHONE EXCHANGE
Birmingham, Michigan
Late 1940s

This is the building that local suburbanites protested when Yamasaki, still at Smith, Hinchman & Grylls, designed it in a conservative northern suburb of Detroit. Designed originally as a two-story structure to be added on to later, the building is unapologetically modernist, simple and functional. Note how Yama extended the second floor out beyond the ground level a bit to allow for a covered walkway and landscaping. Plazas, gardens, water features, and the like were not frills for Yama, but part of the essence of his vision.

Yamasaki gave this telephone exchange building in suburban Birmingham a Bauhaus simplicity but included a covered walkway screened with greenery. This is the project locals protested as ugly. (Photo by John Gallagher)

FEDERAL RESERVE ANNEX
Detroit, Michigan
1951

Crafted while Yama was chief designer for Smith, Hinchman & Grylls, the Federal Reserve Annex delivered a shock of the new to the dowdy Detroit architectural scene. Here at last was the bold statement of the modernist creed—a tall building with a glass curtain wall (Detroit's first) so clean and pure that it speaks in a modest voice amid the cacophony of downtown. Here also was one of Yama's first exterior plazas, the feature that would become a notable part of his work later. To achieve it, Yama set the building back from the street about thirty feet, leaving room for planters with vegetation and a small seating area for office workers and passersby who needed a break from their busy schedules. The Federal Reserve Annex offers a needed caution to those who try to pigeon-hole an architect's work in a single category: Yama would go on to design many other tall buildings, most of which fall more into the category of New Formalism, with extensive use of white stone exteriors and strongly vertical geometry. Here, the Federal Reserve Annex offers but one example of Yama's evolving design palette.

The modern Federal Reserve building in downtown Detroit, with the smaller classical-inspired original building. This was one of Yama's early triumphs and opened a path for modernism in the city. (Photo by John Gallagher)

SLOAN CLINIC
Detroit, Michigan
1953

Early on in his independent career, Yama and his partners were doing all sorts of smaller projects, including this dental clinic on Detroit's east side. Projects like this, along with the many schools, houses, and commercial projects he took on, helped his young firm get its footing while Yama built his reputation as one of architecture's up-and-coming designers.

This modest dentist's office in Detroit was the sort of smaller commission that Yama worked on early in the life of his own firm. (Photo courtesy of Jeffrey Ligan)

UNIVERSITY LIGGETT SCHOOL
Grosse Pointe Woods, Michigan
1954

Oh, to have been there in 1954 to hear how Grosse Pointers reacted when this private school hired the celebrated modernist Minoru Yamasaki to add onto their ivy-covered Colonial-style school! Yama's commission was to add a new lower and middle school along with a library, gym, and other facilities. His classroom buildings, low slung and approached through covered walkways, were something new in the area, and probably a bit shocking to local sensibilities. Even today, on the school's website, the "History" section includes a shot of the traditional 1928 building rather than Yama's work.

University Liggett School, Grosse Pointe Woods, Michigan. (Photo by John Gallagher)

S. BROOKS AND FLORENCE BARRON HOUSE
Detroit, Michigan
1955

Yama accepted all sorts of commissions in the early years of his independent firm, including private residences, which he mostly gave up later on when he started working on skyscrapers. Yama's decision to forego houses for bigger commissions is regrettable, since some of his private residences are delightful. As with the Barron House, his homes frequently offer little to see from the street, often just a low-pitched roof and a screen of brick or landscaping. The magic happens in the interior, which here is marked by travertine and carpeted floors and skylights, all wrapped around a courtyard that features a rectangular pond with aquatic plants. Yama designed this house not long after his return from his 1954 round-the-world trip, during which he saw and learned so much from Asian models. It appears he applied some of what he learned about creating serene interior spaces here. The Barrons were serious collectors of modern American art, and their house became a showroom for works by Claes Oldenburg, Andy Warhol, and many others. The architecture itself, of course, was also a work of art.

Barron House, Detroit, Michigan. (Photo by John Gallagher.)

Another view of the Barron House. (Photo by Rob Yallop; courtesy of the Michigan State Historic Preservation Office)

Interior courtyard of the Barron House. (Photo by Rob Yallop; courtesy of the Michigan State Historic Preservation Office)

BIRMINGHAM UNITARIAN CHURCH
Bloomfield Hills, Michigan
1956

This modest religious structure resembles many of the schools and residences that Yamasaki was creating around this time. There is the same assemblage of single-story Miesian horizontal boxes clustered around a central garden/plaza. Nowhere to be found are the normal elements of church design; there is no steeple, no soaring nave. It was an appropriately modest design for a religious community that offers more questions than answers about faith, a people who considered themselves more choosing than chosen. Yama's work here is quite fine; the slim white steel support columns evoke delicate natural forms, like the stem of a rose or the bone structure of a bird, shapes that Yama often cited as inspiration.

Birmingham Unitarian Church. (Photos by John Gallagher)

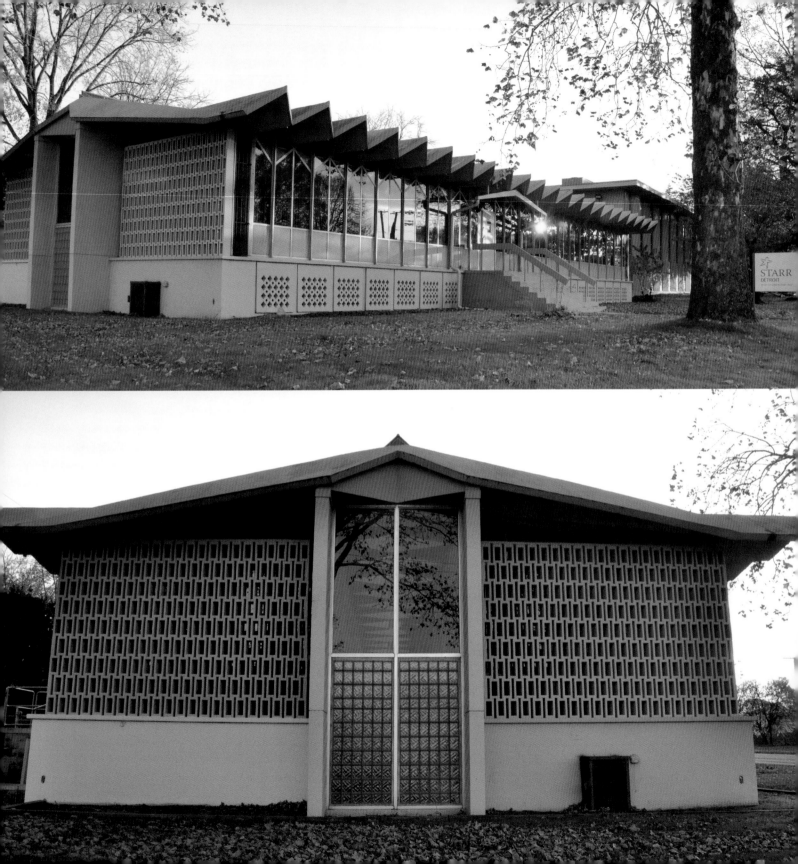

AMERICAN CONCRETE INSTITUTE
Detroit, Michigan
1958

Built for the former American Concrete Institute, a client in whom Yamasaki took great interest because of his appreciation for precast concrete's malleability, this jewel-like little building shows Yama at his mid-career best. Located on West Seven Mile Road in Detroit, this small one-story office structure features many of the motifs that Yama used on many other notable buildings. Offices flank a central sky-lit corridor that runs the length of the building, as at McGregor and the Arts and Crafts Building, and the first floor is raised some four feet above grade just as Yama placed other notable structures—McGregor, for example—on a pedestal for greater visual impact. Precast concrete panels screen the lower portion of the curtain wall and the basement windows, while a similar screen of concrete pipe sections create interest and privacy on the ends. The cantilevered saw-tooth roof pattern was a typical midcentury modern theme. Since Yama's day there have been a few changes; an addition has been respectfully added to one side and a low concrete-block wall that surrounded the building has been removed. Yama's buildings often photographed beautifully, as in this case.

American Concrete Institute. (Photo by John Gallagher)

American Concrete Institute side view. (Photo by John Gallagher)

MCGREGOR MEMORIAL CONFERENCE CENTER
Wayne State University, Detroit, Michigan
1958

Commissioned about the time Yama returned from his 1954 round-the-world journey of discovery, the McGregor Memorial Conference Center shows the architect putting all he had learned to good use. Of all his buildings, this may come closest to embodying the vision he tried throughout his career to achieve, that place of serenity and delight that he talked of so frequently. It helped, of course, that there was plenty of money behind the project; never underestimate the role of a good budget in architectural excellence. It also helped that Yamasaki had created Wayne State University's campus plan about the time he started working on McGregor. Perhaps that gave him a sense of ownership with this project more than with most of his others. It shows.

Interior of McGregor Memorial Conference Center, Wayne State University. (Photo by John Gallagher)

McGregor Memorial Conference Center,
Wayne State University.
(Photo by John Gallagher)

MEYER AND ANNA PRENTIS BUILDING
Wayne State University, Detroit, Michigan
1958

The mid- to late 1950s saw Yamasaki developing his ideas of practical ornamentation and the play of light and shadow, and his cluster of buildings for Wayne State University provided a proving ground for Yama to work out these notions. This three-story office and classroom building was built to house the School of Business Administration. Here, as at the nearby DeRoy Auditorium and McGregor Center, Yama tries to soften and lend a human touch to the otherwise Miesian glass box with plazas and landscaping. In this iteration of his themes, Yama projects the upper two stories outward beyond the ground floor, allowing for a covered walkway. Light-colored travertine stone covers the columns while precast concrete faces the upper two stories. The thin square columns rise to become dividers for the banks of narrow windows on the upper floors. Yama creates, in lieu of his more typical central corridor with a skylight, a broad walk-through passageway. This ground-floor passageway, set slightly off-center, allows passersby on Cass Avenue to glimpse the DeRoy Auditorium; viewers from Prentis get to see the main Detroit Public Library. Yama thus demonstrates his acute awareness of what people not just in his buildings but near them will experience as a result of his artistic choices.

The Meyer and Anna Prentis Building, Wayne State University. (Photo by John Gallagher)

ARTS AND CRAFTS BUILDING (COLLEGE OF CREATIVE STUDIES)
Detroit, Michigan
1958

This delightful little building was designed during a particularly fruitful period in Yama's career, and it shows him at his best. The rather simple plan recalls that of the McGregor Memorial Conference Center a few blocks away. Here Yama crafted a two-story, glass-and-metal-clad building with a central passage running the length of the building and topped with a skylight. Then he buffered the building with adroit landscaping and enclosed the entire composition with an intricate brick screen wall. The result is an oasis for art students and faculty amid a bustling Midtown scene. Those who contend that Yamasaki's smaller buildings are generally better than his much larger commissions can point to McGregor and Arts and Crafts to bolster their case.

The entry to the Arts and Crafts Building, now part of the College for Creative Studies, Detroit, Michigan. (Photo by John Gallagher)

The quiet little garden Yama created at the Arts and Crafts building in Detroit. (Photo by John Gallagher)

REYNOLDS METALS REGIONAL SALES OFFICE
Southfield, Michigan
1959

It's easy to see this building's design as a gimmick, an attempt to please a client who was eager to promote the use of aluminum by using aluminum architecturally in every way possible. But in Yama's capable hands, the project rises to the level of art. Here he employed many of his favorite motifs—setting the building on a pedestal for dramatic effect; surrounding it with a water feature and landscaping; topping the building with a pyramidal- or diamond-inspired skylight; opening the central core of the building for spiritual breathing space; and softening the exterior with an intricately patterned grille. Inside and out, doors, window sashes, gratings, column covers, and many other parts were aluminum. Yamasaki's innovative internal systems, including hot and cold air passages and under-the-floor electrical and telephone ducts, presaged more modern systems to come. Yama was a lifelong innovator, even as he did his best to please the client.

Through the lens of master photographer and Yamasaki friend Balthazar Korab, Yama's Reynolds Metals building in suburban Detroit glows with magic. (Photo by Balthazar Korab; courtesy of the Library of Congress)

Yama's cherished motifs appear even in his starkly commercial buildings—setting a building on a pedestal for dramatic effect and adding water features and landscaping for a connection with nature. (Photo by Balthazar Korab; courtesy of the Library of Congress)

Bathed in natural light from window walls and skylight, Yama's Reynolds Metals building glows with elegance. (Photo by Balthazar Korab, courtesy of the Library of Congress)

MICHIGAN STATE MEDICAL SOCIETY BUILDING
East Lansing, Michigan
1959

The architectural profession dubbed Yamasaki and Edward Durell Stone's style the New Formalism for their adoption of geometric regularity and gleaming white facades, features that seemed to mimic classical buildings. We can see how the tag fits at the Michigan State Medical Society Building, where thirty-one semicircular precast concrete arches rest atop the slender concrete columns that support them. This structure allows for large glass windows on both the front and rear facades. The march of the tall arches across the entire face of the building strikes some as repetitive; others see it as an elegant solution to the problem of light and structure in a modern office building.

Michigan State Medical Society Building. (Photo courtesy of the Michigan State Historic Preservation Office)

COLLEGE OF EDUCATION
Wayne State University, Detroit, Michigan
1960

It is interesting to see how Yama, designing four buildings for Wayne State University all within a few short years and each just steps from the others, worked out his themes in various ways. Here Yama emphasizes the Gothic arch that he liked both aesthetically and for its strength; indeed, the pointed arches form not only the ground-floor covered walkway but continue higher through the upper stories. The building has been compared to the Doge's Palace on St. Mark's Square in Venice, a place that had greatly impressed Yama on his 1954 world tour. More whimsically, some have likened the Education Building to a wedding cake. The story goes that Yama, playing with that idea, placed a tiny wedding-cake bride and groom atop the model of the building he presented to the Wayne State Board of Governors.

Education Building, Wayne State University. (Photo by John Gallagher)

MICHIGAN CONSOLIDATED GAS COMPANY (ONE WOODWARD)

Detroit, Michigan
1963

Yamasaki was no neophyte when it came to tall buildings. During his youthful New York years, one of the firms he worked for, Shreve, Lamb & Harmon, earlier had designed the Empire State Building, and Yama learned a lot at the firm. So when he got the commission to design a new headquarters for the Michigan Consolidated Gas Company in downtown Detroit, one of the first tall-building commissions for his young firm, he was excited and determined to do his very best.

The site alone called for something special. Standing at the foot of Woodward Avenue on the northern edge of Detroit's Civic Center, an assemblage of public buildings, the gas company tower would overlook both the magnificent Detroit River and the new Hart Plaza then in planning. Yama understood the ceremonial power of the site. In its previous headquarters, the gas company had used its lobby as a showroom for appliances powered by gas, but Yama persuaded the company president, Ralph McElvenny, to leave the space open for the public to enjoy. Glass windows that rise to the full ceiling height frame the lobby and create a seamless visual transition to the graceful plaza and plantings that Yama created in front of the building.

This tower saw Yama's first use of narrow windows. It marked a stylistic break with modernism's glass-curtain-wall approach. Yama liked narrow windows in part because he suffered from a fear of heights and thought others did, too, so he wanted windows no wider than an arm span. He also liked the sense of verticality that narrow windows created, running in a delicate latticework up the building. Later he admitted that the effect of "reaching for the sky" diminished the farther one got from the building, but up close his choice emphasized height quite successfully. Yama used precast panels with quartz aggregate on the exterior to create a building that gleams in the sun.

The ceiling lighting in the lobby shows the lengths Yama went to, to realize his vision. His associate Henry Guthard recalled that Yama was fascinated by the little blue flame from a gas jet and wished to somehow express that image as a tribute to his client. So for the lobby ceiling, with a sculptor he admired and often employed, Lee DuSell, he created a series of square elements in which small bulbs shone through blue Plexiglas globes. The

Here Yamasaki transforms the lobby of the Michigan Consolidated Gas Company tower in downtown Detroit from an ordinary commercial space to a glistening work of art. (Photo by Balthazar Korab; courtesy of the Library of Congress)

One of the first of Yama's many tall buildings, and one of the finest. (Photo by John Gallagher)

tiny blue globes were held in place by an X-frame of anodized aluminum that was highly polished. Plexiglas was chosen for the globes rather than glass because the refractive qualities of Plexiglas would bend the light just the right way. "It just turned out to be perfect," Guthard said. In later years, the special bulbs were replaced with more ordinary stock that failed to cast the light the right way, so the effect was lost, but businessman Dan Gilbert of Quicken Loans, who now owns the building, has been working to restore the original type of bulb and taking other steps, including cleaning the exterior, to return the building to pristine condition.

Yama went on to design many tall buildings, in cities as varied as Los Angeles, Seattle, Minneapolis, Madrid, and of course New York, where he created the World Trade Center. But his best expression of the tall building idea may have been achieved at One Woodward Avenue.

The exterior of the Michigan Consolidated Gas building (now One Woodward) shows the repeated geometric patterns that Yamasaki used again and again. (Photo by John Gallagher)

DEROY AUDITORIUM
Wayne State University, Detroit, Michigan
1964

This little jewel box of a building offers a surprisingly expansive space inside, where lectures and other events find a companionable venue. As at nearby McGregor Memorial Conference Center, Yama created a plaza and pools as part of the overall design. The pools were eventually drained due to technical issues; the university hopes to restore them. (McGregor's pools were restored in recent years.)

DeRoy Auditorium at Wayne State University. (Photo by John Gallagher)

MINORU YAMASAKI AND ASSOCIATES OFFICE
Troy, Michigan
1967

Like any artist, Minoru Yamasaki did the occasional self-portrait. For architects, that means creating buildings for their own personal use, freed of the restrictions that clients impose. Yama built this modest-sized office structure in 1967 to house his own firm after years of renting space in a variety of other locations. For a site, he chose a five-acre farm off Big Beaver Road in north suburban Troy, which in the late '60s was nowhere near as busy and developed as it would become. Yama enhanced the semi-rural setting by adding extensive landscaping and berms, so that his headquarters was all but hidden from the nearby road. Simple in plan, the building looks more Miesian than most of Yama's work, with unadorned exterior walls and glass panels instead of the shimmering white precast concrete and aluminum skins he often favored. Perhaps cost was a factor in the simplicity. Whatever the case, the tranquil setting was signature Yama. He was in his midfifties when he built this, and it's tempting to see here the distillation of his decades-long search for a simple, honest, serene workspace. Regrettably, this gem-like building was demolished in 2014, a victim of development pressures along the busy suburban byway.

The tranquil office that Yamasaki designed for his firm on land in Troy, a building now lost to development. (Photo courtesy Michigan State Historic Preservation Office)

YAMASAKI RESIDENCE
Bloomfield Township, Michigan
1972

This is Yama's second self-portrait, completed a few years after he built his office in Troy, and, like that office, his personal residence looks more Miesian than one might expect. There are the same glass panels and unadorned exterior walls, but once again Yama has tucked his building perfectly into the site, so that the house blends effortlessly into the hilly wooded landscape in a northern suburb of Detroit. As with his office, Yama's extensive use of landscaping enhances the total composition. The interiors are pure simplicity, enhanced by touches of artwork, including a gossamer metallic screen by Yama's friend and collaborator Harry Bertoia that divides the dining area from the living room. Here Yama lived the final fourteen or so years of his life, after twenty-five years in the old farmhouse he bought when he first arrived in Detroit.

After the death of Yama's widow, Teri, the estate sold the house in 1998 to interior designer Lynda Charfoos and her family, who have lavished the same loving care on it as Yama did. As Lynda Charfoos tells it:

When I first bought the house, I spent three months walking the house because I was so intimidated to touch it. It was so pure and so clean. I knew I had to do some work. I knew I had to redo the kitchen. But how do you touch an iconic building like this? So I walked it and walked it and looked at the details and tried to figure out why it was the way it was. Why do you feel the way you do when you come in here? Why did he do what he did? I read about him. I interviewed [former Yama associate] Bill Ku. He was very insightful in helping me walk through the changes. In that process of self-discovery I learned what great iconic design is all about. So I have taken that into my practice, and I reap the benefits every single day.

Exterior of the Yamasaki residence in Bloomfield Township, Michigan. (Photo by Rob Yallop; courtesy of the Michigan State Historic Preservation Office)

TEMPLE BETH EL
Bloomfield Township, Michigan
1974

Yamasaki's first important religious structure was North Shore Congregation Israel's synagogue, commissioned in 1959 and completed in 1964 north of Chicago along the shore of Lake Michigan. Yama wrote later that before starting design work he attended a High Holy Day service at the congregation's existing site to get a feel for what he was getting into. At North Shore, he crafted a soaring monumental space set in a beautiful natural setting. A few years later, Yama got the commission to design Temple Beth El in Bloomfield Township northwest of Detroit, and again, as in other types of structures, he used what he had learned in earlier work to achieve his goals for his next commission.

Once again, Yama created a vast, uplifting space to capture and nurture the sense of aspiration essential to a religious building. Beth El's outer form is tent-like, reflecting the history of the Jews, whose first synagogues after their flight from Egypt were tents in the desert. Yama and his preferred engineer, John Skilling, gave the building an innovative structure, framing it lengthwise with curved ridge beams at the top supported by pairs of poured-in-place concrete columns. A skylight runs the length of the sanctuary, while a sophisticated steel-cable system supports the lead-coated copper roof.

In the spacious interior, Yama repeated an ingenious device he had used at North Shore to accommodate both the normal number of those attending a service and the much greater number on High Holy Days. The central area with permanent seating holds about one thousand congregants, while to either side slightly raised platforms can be filled with chairs on holy days to accommodate another eight hundred. By building in room for extra seating, Yama eliminated the awkward schemes used in many religious buildings that deal with overflow crowds by packing them into social halls and the like.

Yama's and Skilling's structural innovations allowed for a ring of windows low to the ground around the entire structure, affording views of the surrounding landscape. That was important to an architect who didn't necessarily share the specific theology of his clients. "Yama was a little bit iffy about Christianity and Judaism

Temple Beth El, Birmingham, Michigan. (Photo by Balthazar Korab; courtesy of the Library of Congress)

and all the rest of it, but he was connected to nature," said Kip Serota, a longtime designer in Yama's office. "And in all of those structures when you're sitting there you have, at eye level, nature on both sides. . . . In all those religious structures you have this connection. If you just turn your head a little bit, nature's right there."

"As in most of Yama's work, you can see a continuum," Henry Guthard, Yama's longtime associate, said. "So you can't look at Temple Beth El without realizing how it started with North Shore Congregation Israel. And you can see how Yama would modify, improve, change, but keep the basic qualities that made his buildings work probably as well as anybody's including Mies van der Rohe."

Interior of Temple Beth El, Birmingham, Michigan. (Photo by Balthazar Korab; courtesy of the Library of Congress)

RAINIER TOWER
Seattle, Washington
1977

At first glance, a viewer wonders how this skyscraper doesn't topple over, so narrow is its base. Locals call it the "beaver building" for its fancied resemblance to a tree gnawed by a beaver. Others have likened it to a golf tee. By going for this unusual structural solution, building a skyscraper atop an eleven-story pedestal base that widens as it rises, Yama left more room at street level for shopping and pedestrian strolling space. It is a dramatic illustration of Yama's structural innovation; critics who said he did nothing more than put a frilly screen around his buildings never gave him credit for his inventiveness in all aspects of architecture.

Rainier Tower in Seattle, the sort of tall-building commission Yama received in the wake of his World Trade Center work. (Photo by Balthazar Korab; courtesy of the Library of Congress)

NOTES

Page 1: The story of Yamasaki's early life is taken from his autobiography: Minoru Yamasaki, *A Life in Architecture* (New York: Weatherhill, 1979), 9–10.

Page 2: **Yama was the hope of his family** Henry Guthard: Author interview.

Page 2: **I almost exploded with excitement** Yamasaki, *A Life in Architecture*, 10–11.

Page 3: **insane . . . impulsive** Yamasaki, *A Life in Architecture*, 15.

Page 4: **first experience with overdrinking** Yamasaki, *A Life in Architecture*, 18.

Page 4: **lessons of those summers** Yamasaki, *A Life in Architecture*, 17.

Page 6: **as deceptively serene as a sunning panther** Russell Bourne, "American Architect Yamasaki," *Architectural Forum*, August 1958.

Page 6: **in addition to his artistic skill** Francis Keally letter is found with other Yamasaki correspondence in the Yamasaki Papers, Walter P. Reuther Library, Wayne State University.

Page 6: **my work has brought me into constant contact** Yamasaki Papers, Walter P. Reuther Library, Wayne State University.

Page 6: **a keen understanding** April 10, 1940, letter by Francis Keally, Yamasaki Papers, Walter P. Reuther Library, Wayne State University.

Page 7: **vivid red gown** Jane Schermerhorn, "The Yamasakis: The Story of a Love Reborn," *Detroit News*, Sept. 7, 1969.

Page 7: The anecdotes of the discrimination Yamasaki suffered during the war can be found in Yamasaki, *A Life in Architecture*, 20–21.

Page 8: **we were anxious to retain your services** Feb. 1, 1944, letter by Leopold Arnaud, dean of architecture of Columbia University, Yamasaki Papers, Walter P. Reuther Library, Wayne State University.

Page 8: **I find a few moments of complete happiness** Yamasaki's brief journal and other personal writings, Yamasaki Papers, Walter P. Reuther Library, Wayne State University.

Page 8: Drafts of *A Life in Architecture* can be found in Yamasaki Papers, Walter P. Reuther Library, Wayne State University.

Page 11: **rare combination of efficiency and monumentality** *Architectural Forum*, February 1947, 78–87. No author listed.

Page 11: **hot dog stand architecture** Yamasaki letter, Jan. 3, 1950, Yamasaki Papers, Walter P. Reuther Library, Wayne State University.

Page 13: **never permitted to meet with the client** Quoted in Thomas J. Holleman and James P. Gallagher, *Smith, Hinchman & Grylls: 125 Years of Architecture and Engineering, 1853–1978* (Detroit: Wayne State University Press, 1978), 149.

Page 15: **man is a ground animal** From an undated speech in Yamasaki Papers, Walter P. Reuther Library, Wayne State University.

Page 15: **one of the sorriest mistakes** Rick Ratliff and John Dunphy, "Troy's World-Class Architect Dies," *Detroit Free Press*, Feb. 8, 1986.

Page 15: **one ghastly mistake** Yamasaki, *A Life in Architecture*, 23.

Page 18: **we all disliked the Beaux-Arts system** John Peter, *The Oral History of Modern Architecture* (New York: Harry N. Abrams, 1994), 15.

Page 19: **charcoal sketch** Yamasaki Papers, Walter P. Reuther Library, Wayne State University.

Page 19: **shallow imitations** Yamasaki, *A life in Architecture*, 24.

Page 19: **you know how you remember** Henry Guthard: Author interview.

Page 19: **modern architecture meant battered walls** Peter, *Oral History of Modern Architecture*, 15.

Page 20: **this portends tragedy** Minoru Yamasaki, "Visual Delight in Architecture," *Architectural Record*, November 1955.

Page 20: **until they came out of my ears** Minoru Yamasaki, interview with Virginia Harriman, August 1959, Archives of American Art, Smithsonian Institution.

Page 20: **as I looked I got very excited** August 13, 1959, interview with Yamasaki by Franklin Page, Archives of American Art, Smithsonian Institution.

Page 20: **looking back** Peter, *Oral History of Modern Architecture*, 15.

Page 24: **buildings should have ornament** Peter, *Oral History of Modern Architecture*, 78.

Page 27: **he worked hard and he played hard** Gunnar Birkerts: Author interview.

Page 27: **dangerously dependent** Yamasaki, *A Life in Architecture*, 27-28.

Page 27: **I was a bad boy** Schermerhorn, *Detroit News*.

Page 27: **a celebrated man** James Glanz and Eric Lipton, *City in the Sky: The Rise and Fall of the World Trade Center* (New York: Times Books, 2003), 100.

Page 27 **Yama is big enough** Glanz & Lipton, *City in the Sky*, 100.

Page 29: **I will try to be more of a Japanese wife** Schermerhorn, *Detroit News*.

Page 29: **I'm just going to be nicer** Schermerhorn, *Detroit News*.

Page 29: **a compassionate iron hand** Kip Serota: Author interview.

Page 29: **Yama came up with the idea internally** Gunnar Birkerts: Author interview.

Page 29: **an architect who worked with emotion** Gunnar Birkerts: Author interview.

Page 31: **Yama's presence was ubiquitous** Henry Guthard: Author interview.

Page 31: **I was hired to be an architect** Yamasaki, *A Life in Architecture*, 26.

Page 31: **recalled how he had been fired** John Suhr: Author interview.

Page 31: **he was everywhere** Henry Guthard: Author interview.

Page 32: **the doors, the hinges** Henry Guthard: Author interview.

Page 32: **there was a guy who was very critical** Henry Guthard: Author interview.

Page 34: **gas is best** Yamasaki, *A Life in Architecture*, 53–54.

Page 35: **the manufacturer produces** Yamasaki, interview with Virginia Harriman.

Page 35: **it's very important for the architect** Yamasaki, interview with Virginia Harriman.

Page 36: **Yama came out knowing everything** Henry Guthard: Author interview.

Page 36: **this type of technology** Henry Guthard: Author interview.

Page 38: **a moment of low comedy** Yamasaki, *A Life in Architecture*, 114; and author interviews with Henry Guthard and Kip Serota. See also Glanz & Lipton, *City in the Sky*, 88–117.

Page 41: **doesn't really matter in Manhattan** Yamasaki, *A Life in Architecture*, 113.

Page 41: **great outdoor space** Yamasaki, *A Life in Architecture*, 113.

Page 42: **an outstandingly serious and searching attempt** Ada Louise Huxtable, "N.Y.C. Architectural Ups and Downs," *New York Times*, February 2, 1964.

Page 42: **violently emotional** March 8, 1974, Yamasaki letter to Henry Wright of City College of New York, Yamasaki Papers, Walter P. Reuther Library, Wayne State University.

Page 46: **only the first-time visitor** Yamasaki, *A Life in Architecture*, 113.

Page 46: **Manhattan's Tower of Babel** Glanz & Lipton, *City in the Sky*, 116.

Page 46: **towers are pure technology** Huxtable column: *New York Times*, April 5, 1973. Reprinted in Ada Louise Huxtable, *Kicked a Building Lately* (Quadrangle/The New York Times Book Co., 1976), New York, N.Y., 122–23.

Page 46: Yamasaki response to Huxtable letter dated April 10, 1973, Yamasaki Papers, Walter P. Reuther Library, Wayne State University.

Page 49: **a paved garden** Russell Lynes, "The Architect Was Told 'World Trade' So He Planned Big," *Smithsonian*, January 1978, 43.

Page 49: **as another master** Huxtable, "Princeton Institute: At the Head of Its Class," reprinted in *Kicked a Building Lately*, 89.

Page 50: **twittering aviary** Quoted in Glanz & Lipton, *City in the Sky,* 100.

Page 50: **as much an architect as I am Napoleon** Quoted in Glanz & Lipton, *City in the Sky,* 100.

Page 50: **mere artistic caprice** Quoted in Glanz & Lipton, *City in the Sky,* 100.

Page 50: **cover them with frilly decorations** Roddy Ray and Marsha Miro, "Minoru Yamasaki: Architect a 'Sensitive Creator,'" *Detroit Free Press*, Feb. 9, 1986; 1.

Page 50: **ornament was still a crime** Eric Hill: Author interview.

Page 50: Philip Johnson letter, March 29, 1956, Yamasaki Papers, Walter P. Reuther Library, Wayne State University.

Page 53: **I had not known about McGregor** Eric Hill: Author interview.

Page 56: **in order to believe in God** Temple Beth El dedication brochure, Yamasaki Papers, Walter P. Reuther Library, Wayne State University.

Page 56: Drafts of *A Life in Architecture*, Yamasaki Papers, Walter P. Reuther Library, Wayne State University.

Page 56: **just plain bad** Yamasaki, *A Life in Architecture*, 36.

Page 58: **the way we imagine an architect to be** Gunnar Birkerts: Author interview.

Page 58: **Yama always taught us** Henry Guthard: Author interview.

Page 95: **it just turned out to be perfect** Henry Guthard: Author interview.

Page 100: **when I first bought the house** Lynda Charfoos: Author interview.

Page 103: **a little bit iffy** Kip Serota: Author interview.

Page 104: **you can see a continuum** Henry Guthard: Author interview.

INDEX

American Concrete Institute, 74–75

Arts and Crafts Building, 82–83

Barron House, 68–71

Bauhaus, 11, 19, 23

Beaux-Arts, 18, 20, 23

Bertoia, Harry, 100

Birkerts, Gunnar, x–xi, 27, 29, 31, 58

Birmingham Unitarian Church, 72–73

Brown, Keith, xi

Bunshaft, Gordon, 13, 20, 50

Charfoos, Lynda, 100

College of Education Building, ix, 22, 33, 35, 90–91

DeRoy Auditorium, ix, 96–97

DuSell, Lee, 92

Federal Reserve Building, 11, 13, 19, 58, 62–63

Githens and Keally, 6

Guardian Building, 11

Guthard, Henry, xi, 2, 19, 23, 31–32, 35–36, 45, 58, 92, 95, 104

Harrison, Fouilhoux, and Abramovitz, 8

Hellmuth, George, 13

Hill, Eric, xi, 50, 53

Huxtable, Ada Louise, 38, 42, 46, 49

Johnson, Lyndon Baines, 47

Johnson, Philip, 50, 53

Korab, Balthazar, xi, 27

Lambert Airport St. Louis, 13, 15

Lapidus, Morris, 49–50

Leinweber, Joseph, 13, 16

Lever House, 19–20

McGregor Memorial Conference Center, ix, 23–25, 36, 53, 58–59, 76–79

Michigan Bell Telephone Exchange, 11, 19, 60–61

Michigan Consolidated Gas building, 34, 36, 53, 92–95

Michigan State Medical Society Building, 88–89

Mies van der Rohe, Ludwig, 13, 18–20, 24, 36, 49, 58

New Formalism, 49–50, 58

New York Times, 38, 42, 46, 49

One Woodward. *See* Michigan Consolidated Gas building

Pei, I. M., 50

Penobscot Building, 11

Prentis Building, 80–81

Pruitt-Igoe, 15, 17

Rainier Tower, 106–7

Reynolds Metals building, 36, 84–87

Rowland, Wirt, 11

Rudolph, Paul, 50

Sarinen, Eero, 29, 50, 53

Saudi Arabia, 52, 56

Science Pavilion Seattle World's Fair, 36–38, 50

Scully, Vincent, 49

Seattle, x, 1, 36, 50

Serota, Kip, xi, 29, 104

Shreve, Lamb & Harmon, 6–7

Skidmore, Owings and Merrill, 20

Skilling, John, 103

Sloan Clinic, 64–65

Smith, Hinchman & Grylls, 8, 11–13, 16, 18, 19

Stone, Edward Durrell, 49

Suhr, John, xi, 31

Taj Mahal, 20, 58

Temple Beth El, 56, 58, 102–5

Time, 38–39

University Liggett School, 18, 66–67

Wayne State University, ix, xi, 19, 21–25, 33, 35–36, 59, 76–79, 80–81, 90–91, 96–97

World Trade Center, ix-xi, 24, 36, 38–49, 53, 58–59

Yamasaki, Minoru: Alaskan canneries, 3–4; Alcohol use, 4, 27; Beaux-Arts style, 18, 20, 23; Birth, 1; Coming to Detroit, 8, 11; Death, 56; Design philosophy, 18–20, 23–24; Discrimination against, x, 7, 13; Early life, 1–2; Education, 2–4; Health, x, 27, 56; Later years, 53, 56; Marriage, 7, 27–29; Memoirs, x-xi, 4, 8, 56; Model making, 32, 34, 42; New York City years, 4–10, 41; Personal strife, 27, 29; Physical description, 6; Pruitt-Igoe, 15, 17; Reputation within profession, 49–50, 53;

Smith, Hinchman & Grylls, 8, 11–13, 16, 18, 19; Starting own firm, 13; Use of materials, 34–36; Watercolors and drawing, vi, 5–6, 8, 10; Wayne State University, ix, xi, 19, 21–25, 33, 35–36, 59, 76–79, 80–81, 90–91, 96–97; World Trade Center, ix-xi, 36, 38–49, 53, 58–59; World War II, 7–9

Yamasaki, Teruko (Teri), 7, 14, 27–29, 56, 100

Yamasaki & Associates building, 56, 98–99

Yamasaki residence, 54–56, 100–101